SQUAMISH WHISTLER
MOUNTAINBIKE TRAIL GUIDE

Rob Cocquyt
Dave Kelly

Elaho Publishing Corporation
Squamish BC

Squamish—Whistler Mountainbike Trail Guide

© Rob Cocquyt and Dave Kelly 1997

Maps © Kevin McLane.

ISBN 0-9696201-7-9

Elaho Publishing Corporation, Squamish BC.

Printed in Canada by Kromar Printing Ltd, Winnipeg, Manitoba.

Front cover : Warren Scott and Lynn McLane nearing the top of the Cheakamus Canyon Trail.   Photo: Kevin McLane.

Back cover : Lost Lake Trails. Photo: Elisabeth Swan, Coast Mountain Photography
Kelvin Biberdorf on Five Point Hill.   Photo: Kevin McLane.

Canadian Cataloguing in Publication Data

Cocquyt, Rob 1970-
Kelly, Dave 1971-
  Squamish—Whistler Mountainbike Trail Guide
  Includes index.
  1. All terrain cycling--British Columbia--Squamish--Guidebooks.
  2. All terrain cycling--British Columbia--Whistler--Guidebooks.
  3. Trails--British Columbia--Squamish--Guidebooks.
  4. Trails--British Columbia--Whistler--Guidebooks.
  5. Squamish (BC)--Guidebooks.
  6. Whistler (BC)--Guidebooks.
  II. Title
  GV1046.C32B75 1997   796.6'3'0971131   C97-910266-9

ALL RIGHTS RESERVED

This book and all maps contained are copyrighted. Other than brief quotations in reviews, no part of this book may be reproduced in any form, or by electronic, mechanical, or any other means without written permission from the publisher.

PRIVATE PROPERTY

Descriptions to trails which may lie, in part, on undeveloped private land indicate historical usage only—they do not imply public right of access. Please observe any posted signage.

NOW READ THIS!

Mountainbiking is a potentially hazardous activity carrying a significant risk of personal injury, and should only be undertaken with a full understanding of all inherent risks. This book is only a guide to the trails, a composite of opinions from many sources, some of which may not be accurate and the information contained may not reflect the circumstances of a particular trail on a given day. **This guide must always be used in conjunction with the exercise of experience, tuition, and careful judgement.**

Table of Contents — 1

Regional Map .... Inside front cover
Acknowledgements 7
Introduction 8
How To Use This Guide 10
Trail Grading 11
On the Trail 12
Code of Conduct, Useful Phone Numbers 13
Tools, Tubes and Torments, Riding Safely 14
WORCA & SORCA, Loonie Races 15
Trail Building 16
Natural Hazards 17

- SQUAMISH -

Squamish Area Map 18
Introduction 19
First Glance 21
Recommended Rides 22-23
Facilities 24
Trail Ownership 25
Squamish Estuary - Malamute Map 26
Squamish Estuary - Malamute Trails 27
The Smoke Bluffs Map 28
The Smoke Bluffs Trails 29-30
Crumpit Woods Map 32
Crumpit Woods Trails 31-33
Ring Creek South Map 34
Ring Creek South Trails 35
Ring Creek North Map 36
Ring Creek North Trails 37-39
Garibaldi Highlands Map 40
Garibaldi Highlands Trails 41
Alice Lake Map 42
Alice Lake Trails 43
Cheekye Fan Map 46
Cheekye Fan Trails 47
Cat Lake Map 48
Cat Lake Trails 49-51
Brohm Lake Map 52
Brohm Lake Trails 53
Cheakamus Canyon Map 54
Cheakamus Canyon Trails 55
Chance Creek - Function Junction & Elfin Lakes Maps 56
Chance Creek - Function Junction Trails 57

Table of Contents — 2

- WHISTLER -

Whistler Area Map 58
Introduction 59
First Glance 61
Recommended Rides 62-63
Facilities 64
Trail Ownership 65
Upper Cheakamus Valley Map 66
Upper Cheakamus Valley Trails 67-69
Creekside to the Village Map 70
Creekside to the Village Trails 71-73
Village to Green Lake Map 74
Village to Green Lake Trails 75-77
West Side South Map 78
West Side North Map 80
West Side Trails 79-83
Green Lake — Shadow Lake Map 84
Green Lake — Shadow Lake Trails 85

Squamish Tick List 87-89
Whistler Tick List 90-91
Night Riding 93
Test of Metal Race Map 94
Cheakamus Challenge Race Map 95
Some Trail Origins 96

———————— § ————————

Acknowledgements

This guide is a compendium of knowledge drawn from the minds and efforts of many helpful people. Those listed below had a direct and profound influence on the contents of this book whether it be through their knowledge of local wisdom, or their sharp editorial skills.

Mike "Neighbour" Boothroyd	Jane Graham	Kevin McLane
The trials guys	Craig Kauszman	Lynn McLane
Holly Briand	Paul Kindree	Cliff Miller
Ron Enns	Marika Koenig	Stu Pinkney
Jamie Grant	Genevieve Leger	Paul "Rolo" Rawlinson
Al Grey	Bob Lorriman	Al Ross
Dave Heisler	Trent "P-Nut" Lynn	Mike Rothdram
Armand Hurford	Ken "Fencepost" Marler	Chris Runnals

Next come many dedicated and hard working people who have committed more than their fair share of time toward trail development and maintenance. Without their efforts, most of the trails in this guide simply would not exist.

Larry Allen	Armand Hurford	Paul "Rolo" Rawlinson
Marc Armour	Craig Kauszman	Grey Rodier
Don Barnes	Ross Kirkwood	Mike Rothdram
Kelvin Biberdorf	Troy Lynn	Warren "War Dog" Scott
Jim Bowes	Ken "Fencepost" Marler	Ross Smith
Ray Christianson	Grant "G-Man" Martin	Chris Staats
Jamie Coleman	George McIntosh	Dan "Danimal" Swanstrom
Brennan Covey	Kevin McLane	Glenn "Busby" Thompson
Dale Douglas	Cliff Miller	John Tisdale
Brian Goldstone	Dick Parker	Brad Walkey
Ed Green	Ray Peters	Larry Wedge
Al Grey	Joe "Sap" Raguero	Eric Wight

The following people have helped made life easier for us during the time that this guide was developed.

Clive Appleby	Ron Goldstone	Nick
Chris Atkinson	Hamish and Margret	Andy Otter
Annie Barnes	Holly	Ann Peters
Bashaw	Jay	Chris Platz
B.T.	Heather and Dirk Of Savory Slice Pizza	Chris Runnals
Tom Bell	Keith McGee	Perry and Becky
BC Parks	Ministry of Forests, Squamish	Jeff Stovin
Corsa Cycles	Ailsa Siemens	Tantalus Bike Shop
Daniel	Pat "No Pat's" Mulhall	Al Woods
Genevieve	The Crew of Local Dirt and People Power Trailblazers	

Special thanks are due to photographers Jamie Grant, Brian Goldstone, Bonny Makarewicz, Kevin McLane, Elisabeth Swan and Guillaume Tessier. And finally, a very special thank-you is deserved to Grant Lamont and Charlie Doyle for their previous guidebook work on Whistler, and Terra-pro GPS surveys.

Introduction

This book, with one hundred and thirty five trails described, is aimed at anyone who rides a bike and wishes to expand their fat-tire universe into the Squamish and Whistler area. It covers all the best trails, the worst trails and everything in between.

This is not Moab nor Crested Butte nor Rossland nor Marin County—it is Sea To Sky Country on the coast of British Columbia, just an hour or two hour north of Vancouver. This is a land of high mountains, clouds, rain and sun; old growth forests of ancient trees; cold glacial rivers and slugs the size of hot dogs; steep granite slabs; mellow riverside spins; breathtaking views reached by breathtaking climbs. This is roots and rocks and mud and moss, cool clear lakes and pine-needle covered trails—this is why we live here.

Although generally considered to be one big region, Squamish and Whistler actually have quite different characteristics. Elevation, for example: Whistler is at 700 metres in the valley and 60 kilometres inland, whereas Squamish starts at sea-level. Consequently, Whistler is colder in winter, warmer in summer and has a shorter season due to snow. On the trails, Squamish tends to have more of the roots—Whistler more of the rocks.

Mountain biking in this region is still in its infancy. A handful of locals have been riding some of these trails for years but never has there been so much energy directed towards exploring, building and maintenance as in recent years, as more people discover the profound satisfaction derived from riding in this magnificent terrain. The future holds great promise too, with potential alpine links over the ridges from valley to valley.

Could we have kept all this a secret? Yes. Should we have kept this all a secret? No. With the ever expanding metropolis of Vancouver just a short drive away and Whistler, the world class four season resort on the northern boundary, the "secret" was already out. Nevertheless, the decision to spill the beans required careful thought and consideration. Previously, only

INTRODUCTION

a handful of trails were known to those outside the mountain biking communities in Squamish and Whistler. The best trails were intensively ridden and suffered damage and erosion from over-use whilst many others were rarely travelled, forgotten, or overgrown to the point of being unridable. With any luck this guide, with so many trails to choose from, will spread riders around and encourage exploration of the new, the different and the more obscure areas tucked away in the corners of Squamish and Whistler.

Riders who are very familiar with the area may notice a few trails missing from these pages. This is not an oversight, but rather an attempt to steer people away from trails on developed private property, very severe erosion problems, especially sensitive user conflicts, or a clear directive that bikes are not welcome. All were considered justifiable reasons for exclusion.

Both Squamish and Whistler are growing rapidly and this will inevitably lead to the loss of some trails as development moves onward. Given that Squamish, as well as Whistler is now an international centre for adventure recreation pursuits like hiking, cycling, skiing and climbing, the wise developer is more attuned than in the past to the potential benefits of a well-planned trail system, and increasingly, excellent trail networks are being worked into development plans.

On the subject of dreams, it may one day be possible to ride on trails entirely from Squamish, northward to D'Arcy, a distance of about 150 kilometres, without ever having to cruise the blacktop. Many people have invested significant amounts of time and money towards achieving that goal. The Sea-To-Sky-Trail, as it is known, while still more of a vision than a tangible earthen track, may yet become a reality one day.

Welcome to our playground.

Rob Cocquyt, Dave Kelly

May 1st 1997

How To Use This Guide

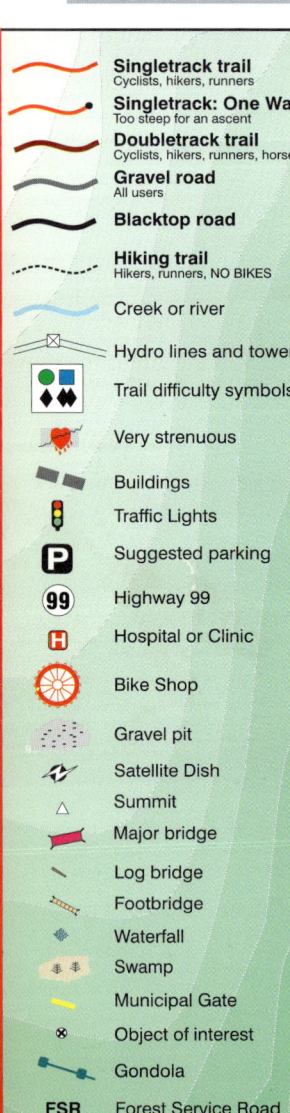

Trails in this guide are all numbered consecutively from 1 to 136, to help with quick reference on both maps and text descriptions. The guide describes individual areas in logical order from south to north. Each map generally tries to follow that pattern too.

The Grading System... Trails are grading according to four levels of technical difficulty. A fifth grade shows those trails which are especially strenuous.

Using the maps... The maps are best considered to be "Infographics", and as such, are not to scale and contain only information pertinent to the trails and finding your way around. The Trail Index Boxes on each map list the numbers and grades of all the trails shown within that map area, which may overlap with adjacent areas.

Trail Networks... There are several very popular networks of trails in the Whistler area which are too complex to describe in detail. They are noted by a background as shown here.

To find a map... The fastest way to find a particular map is to look it up in the Table of Contents.

To find a trail.. The fastest way to get information on a specific trail, or to look for rides in a particular grade, is to look up the trail number and page in the Tick List at the back of the book.

Trail Grading

Trail grading is a very subjective affair, dependent as much on the state of mind of the rider as the terrain. **The grades applied in this guide, Easy, Moderate, Difficult and Very Difficult apply only to the technical difficulty of staying upright on the bike.** High speed is another matter, as is the amount of energy output. You have "successfully" ridden the trail when your face breaks into a smile or laughter escapes your lips.

Lifting the bike over an intimidating obstacle, or choosing to walk down a steep pitch are also a normal part of the game. In that regard, it is worth considering that some of the harder trails in this guide are so good, it is worth taking the time to accept a little more hike-a-biking in order to enjoy the fun stuff.

Easy... ● Expect few if any obstacles and a generally good surface to the trail. Suitable for beginners, the timid, just about any kind of bike with fat tires, little kids, or experienced riders who want a stress-free pedal.

Moderate... ■ Most trails will have some combination of rough surface, hand built obstacles, natural obstacles, tight bends, mud holes, roots and rocks. Short steep sections that would be at home on a Difficult trail are possible too. Just about any fit rider can have lots of fun on these trails.

Difficult... ◆ Obstacles will be much bigger and more numerous, or the downhill will be way steeper. Or both. Falling off in the wrong place will usually result in more blood than a Moderate trail. Cleaning trails (no dabs!) at this grade requires a high level of bike skill. You can always walk.

Very Difficult... ◆◆ The hardest trails for the honed and the bold. Usually very steep, involving a risk of serious falls, breaking more than the bike in the process. Stay away unless you get bored cleaning Difficult trails time after time.

♥ ... Especially strenuous rides, involving lots of climbing and many hours on the trail—not likely to appeal to you unless you are very fit. Such rides usually have very little technical difficulty, but encompass some of the best outings in the guide.

On The Trail

Whistler and Squamish are both very active outdoor communities, where many people frequent the trails. The great majority of trails listed in this guide are essentially urban in nature, close to residential areas or in heavily-used recreation centres. This is not remote backcountry where other users are a rare sight, so leave the rack at home and expect to meet hikers and other cyclists at any time. Few trails are closed to the mountainbike, but those that are, are for good reason. Usually they are narrow and popular traditional hiking trails, and the erosion or collision potential, or both, are very real.

On gravel roads, expect to find logging trucks, recreational vehicles, industrial users, horses and moto-cross bikes. On doubletrack trails (dark red map lines), vehicle access is usually not possible, otherwise expect to find just about any other user. Be especially careful of horses—slow down and give them a respectfully wide berth. Some horses can spook easily, endangering everyone, but they too, like to enjoy their day.

Singletrack is the domain of cyclists, hikers and runners, and to a minor extent, the surprisingly soft touch of motorcycle trials riders. Moto-cross bikes, however, can be very damaging on this kind of soft, narrow terrain. Horses can also be astonishingly destructive on the soft singletrack trails of coastal forests, as any cyclist knows who has to ride through later. Steel shod hooves tear up the trails rapidly and destroy hand built obstacles, and the size of a horse, filling a narrow trail, can make passing problematic for both. And then there is the horseshit, usually smack in the middle of the trail.

There is no doubt that the trail erosion of the last few years as mountainbiking has soared in popularity, is a problem. One bike does little damage. A thousand can. Care, local planning, seasonal closures, and regular trail maintenance programs could do much to alleviate the situation. Given that so many singletrack trails, especially in the Squamish area, have been built by mountainbikers over the last decade, cyclists have much to gain from a pro-active and responsible attitude.

Code of Conduct

Be courteous to other trail users... They want to be there too, and everyone's day is more pleasant with a smile or a wave.

Stay alert at all times... This your best possible defence against injury, bike damage, or collision.

Be prepared for emergencies... Injuries happen. To you.

Respect the land... People will ride these trails long after you have passed on. Leave a legacy of care and quality. Good karma.

Observe trail closures... It will never open again if you don't.

Avoid skidding... Avoid locking your brakes whenever possible. Pick a line, control your speed, and cruise on through.

Heavy rains... Avoid soft trails after heavy rains, especially in winter and spring, to allow drying and minimise erosion.

Avoid unnecessary speed... A mountainbiker attempting to pass at high speed can be an alarming threat to hikers or horses, especially on a popular trail. Save the speed for appropriate places, and always be ready for the unexpected.

Leave no garbage... Always pack out everything that you bring in. Leave only sweat and tire tracks.

Repair the damage... Spend a little time working on the trails occasionally to help repair the erosion you inevitably cause.

Useful Phone Numbers

All numbers are area code 604

BC Forest Service	898-2100
BC Parks	898-3678
Cycling BC	332-1367
Emergency	911

WHISTLER

WORCA	938-9893
Local Weather & Information	932-5090
Resort Municipality of Whistler	932-5535
Meadow Park Sports Centre	938-3133
Whistler tourism information	932-5528
Whistler Police (non-emergency)	932-3044
Whistler Mountain	932-3434
Blackcomb Mountain	932-3141

SQUAMISH

SORCA	898-3519
Local Weather & Information	892-3050
District of Squamish	892-5217
Brennan Park Leisure Centre	898-3604
Squamish tourism information	898-9244
Squamish Police (non-emerg.)	898-9678

BIKE SHOPS

W- Grinders Bikes & Boards	905-2453
W- Whistler Backroads	932-3111
W- Evolution	932-2967
S- Corsa Cycles	892-3331
S- Tantalus Bike Shop	898-2588

14

Tools, Tubes and Torments

Before heading out on the trail, take a moment to think about how you will get back home if: you have no spare tube, pump or tire levers when you get a flat (or two); your chain breaks and you have no chainbreaker; you need to adjust a seat post and you have no allen keys; a spoke breaks and you have no spoke key. Experienced riders don't usually make these mistakes (but they can), inexperienced riders don't know how miserable things can get if tools are not carried.

Hardship can be avoided if your bike is well maintained and runs smoothly. If you don't have all of this essential stuff, head for a bike shop before you ride again. If you do, ask yourself honestly if you really know how to use it. If not, find out quick. It is your insurance policy.

Riding Safely

This is mountain terrain with mountain weather: cold rain in summer, cold mud anytime. Summer heat in the high 30s. Sleet in spring and fall. Rain always. Numerous hazards exist out there in the woods to snare the unwary. If you are uncertain of local characteristics, pedal softly until you learn more. Tell someone where you are going and stick to that plan. Take enough food and water: it is easy to underestimate both on a long ride. Pack a small first aid kit and bike tools. Make sure your bike-handling skills are adequate for your ride, lowering your seat can help. Walking down or over a difficult section is better than getting smacked, but prolonged hike-a-biking can add a lot of time to your ride. Remember that in the trees, darkness falls faster than in open areas. High winds, especially around Squamish, can make the woods surprisingly hazardous due to breaking trees and branches. Always assess your limits, and push them only when the time is right.

Develop good riding style on the trails. Ride with others who are more accomplished. Practising trackstands, wheelies and bunnyhops can be a lot of fun, and some skill at these (and other) techniques helps make your time on the trail more enjoyable, as well as undoubtedly safer.

WORCA & SORCA

Whether you are lucky enough to live in this area and able to ride the trails every day, or are passing through on a road trip, give some thought to joining one or both of the local bike clubs. Your membership dollars are a real contribution toward helping to maintain and preserve access to the trails, and brings good karma (if you are visiting the area for the first time you will soon learn how handy good karma can be!)

The Whistler Off-Road Cycling Association and the Squamish Off-Road Cycling Association help provide a unified local voice to deal with access issues, new trail development and repair, social events and local races and more. Both groups provide newsletters to keep members up to date wherever they may be, and hold membership meetings on a regular basis.

WORCA... Box 3500 - 31, Whistler, BC, V0N 1B0.
Loonie race information hotline 604-938-9893.

SORCA... Box 793, Garibaldi Highlands, BC, V0N 1T0.
Information 604-898-3519.

Loonie Races

Both Whistler and Squamish have a very active local race calendar, running usually from mid-April to October. Known as Loonie Races (the cost of the entry fee), they are mass-start events, usually about forty-five minutes long for the average rider, fast, furious and very sociable occasions. Whistler usually hosts one each week, organised by WORCA and Squamish two per month, organised by the two bike shops alternately, with involvement from SORCA. The Whistler series has enjoyed huge success over the last few years, with mass starts of over a hundred riders now commonplace. Courses vary, usually on Easy to Moderate trails, at popular venues which offer good race terrain. To enter, just show up at the start (early!)

Whistler... Loonie Race hotline 604-938-9893

Squamish... Call either Tantalus Bike Shop 604-898-2588
or Corsa Cycles 604-892-3331

16

Trail Building

Where would we be without trails to ride on? Perhaps we'd all be doomed to skinny tires, cruising up and down Highway 99, begging for wider shoulders. Banish the thought. Trails are the backbone of the fat tire experience and trail building is a task of the highest honour.

If you decide you want to build your first trail, make it a short one. It is much easier to get it finished. It could be a gentle link between existing trails, a challenging plunge, or your own version of obstacle heaven. Before the first swing of the mattock, contact one of the local bike clubs. They are a great source for advice, tools, and volunteer help. They have experience. Check who owns the land. Private developed land should be avoided at all costs. Undeveloped private land is a touchy subject. Unless a trail system has already been established, it is best avoided. If prominent signage has been erected (this does happen) clearly indicating you are not welcome, respect it and stay out. Trails built on private land are temporary at best, examples of here-today, gone-tomorrow.

Much of the significant future trail development in this region will occur on crown land—major links that enable huge loop rides between the valleys and over the ridge tops. Such developments are governed by the Forest Practices Code of BC. Under Code regulations, any new trail development must follow certain procedures and meet established standards. A proposal including the location, length, use, and standards of the trail must be submitted to the Forest Service for approval (get advice from someone who has done this before.) This serves to ensure that the trail you plan to build will not be logged or altered in the foreseeable future. If, at some point in the future road building or logging alters the trail, the Forest Service will take responsiblity for rebuilding or relocating it. Trails which are approved through this process may qualify for full or partial funding for construction and maintenance.

Whether a trail be built with the approval of all the people who count, or built in the light of a full moon in dark clothes, keep in mind that the trail will be your signature. Do it right.

17
Natural Hazards

Water... *Giardia Lamblia* (Beaver Fever) is present in this area. If you really must drink from the trail, a spring or small creek is the best option, but you are taking a chance. Best not to.

Sticks... This area is notorious (Squamish especially) for derailer-eating sticks on trails which are less well travelled, or new—especially in the early spring after winter has left its mark. Keep in mind that the sound of a snapping LX derailer is not nearly so horrifying as that of an XTR.

Bears... Black bears are common. When you encounter one on the trail (and you will) do not try to push your way past. While most bears will eventually run away, many Whistler bears are so accustomed to seeing people that they won't even blink an eye. The best thing to do is turn around and find another trail to pedal. It is not out of the question that you may one day encounter a grizzly bear in one of the more remote areas.

Cougars... These magnificent big cats are a much more elusive than bears, but there are plenty of them around. They are most active at dusk and dawn but will roam and hunt at any time of the day or night. If you come upon a cougar stay calm! Do not approach and do not turn your back. Pick up a stick, move slowly, position your bike between you and it, do everything you can to enlarge your image, such as extending your arms and opening your jacket, and slowly back off. If the cougar attacks, fight back!

The weather... Especially if you have come from a warmer climate, it is wise to learn the ways of local weather. The pacific coastal climate is fickle at best, with generally mild winters, warm summers, and rain always. This place is green.

Squamish has milder temperatures in winter and spring than Whistler, but is usually a little cooler in summer and more prone to strong winds. Whistler is at a higher elevation, about 700 metres in the valley, so the temperature can drop significantly as you climb and rain can come at any time. However, July to September usually sees extended dry spells and temperatures can climb regularly into the 30s.

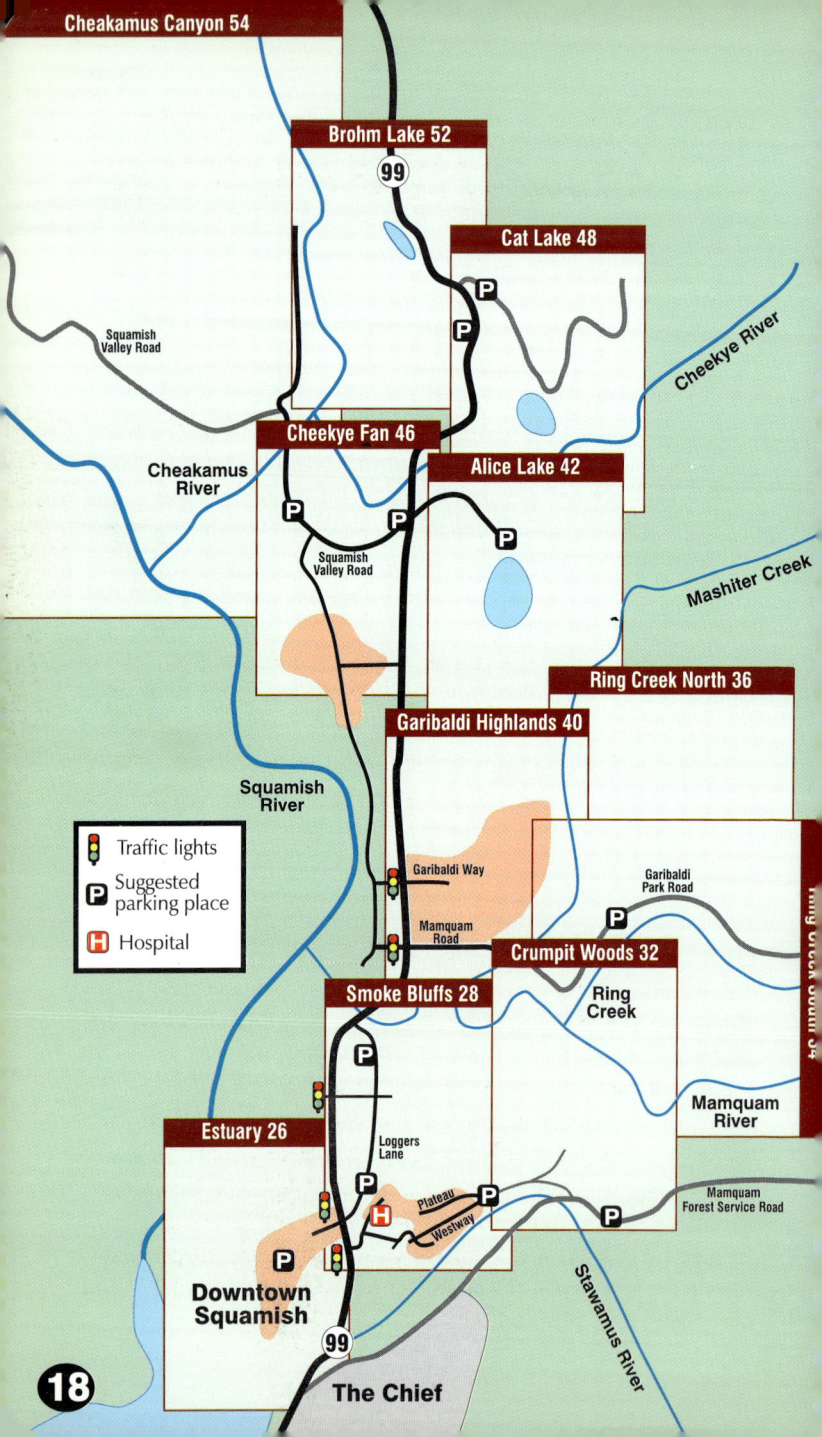

SQUAMISH

Already an international rock climbing destination and a wind surfing mecca where the wind always blows, it is only fitting that Squamish should develop its outstanding potential for an extensive and immensely varied mountain bike trail system. The subtle combination of the mild west coast climate, a location midway between Vancouver and Whistler, the rapid growth of adventure sports in the community, and a vastly increased number of trails over the last few years have now made Squamish a must-ride-there destination high on every mountainbikers wish list.

The wide valley of the Squamish River has an unusually varied mix of terrain, with many small summits offering expansive views of the higher peaks, numerous side valleys which offer quiet exploration, and trails along glacial riversides. Vast networks of overgrown logging roads hug the valley walls, and the legacy of narrow, gentle grades of abandoned logging railroads from the 1930s have proven well suited to a quality trail experience for all abilities.

The riding season usually runs from the onset of the milder temperatures of March to the rains of November, although it is often possible year round on trails low in the valley. Snow and cold temperatures in December and January can effectively put a freeze on riding everywhere for weeks at a time. Many trails tend to be muddy and prone to erosion until the warmer weather of May. All of the trails with the exception of Elfin Lakes and Brohm Ridge should be snow free by the end of April unless the winter has been abnormally harsh.

There are over 80 trails listed in the Squamish area and they cover terrain from the tight singletrack of the valley floor, to the cyclist's autobahn of *The Ring Creek Rip*, and the big sky grandeur of high alpine meadows. Beyond the scope of this guide are hundreds of kilometers of forestry roads which lead deep into the backcountry.

Surprisingly, the vast majority of trails that now exist in the Squamish area have only been developed since 1992. Prior to then, *Jacks Trail*, the *Mashiter Trail*, *The Four Lakes Trail*, *Roller Coaster*, and few others offered singletrack experience. The *Cheakamus Canyon*, *Hut Lake* and *Elfin Lakes* were the primo big rides. Since then, a formidable amount of energy has been directed by cyclists into developing over fifty kilometres of quality singletrack. Some were long overgrown logging roads, resurrected from the forest—a prime example being the *Ring Creek Rip* in 1991—and dozens of others just like *Endo*, *Rusty Bucket*, *Lost Loop* and *Made in the Shade*, all scratched out of the dirt by hand.

The Squamish Off Road Cycling Association came into being in 1992, pioneered by Cliff Miller. Jim Bowes discovered the enchanting landscape of Crumpit Woods around that time, and SORCA members developed *S&M*, *Lost Loop*, *Root 99* and *Meet Yer Maker*. 1994-95 were the years of the Brodie race near Alice Lake, introducing many racers to Squamish for the first time. *Made in the Shade*, and *Cliffs Corners* came to be as a result.

In 1996, the first mass start Test of Metal race on an epic 65 kilometre point to point course generated a major amount of difficult trail development, and demonstrated the potential of Squamish to a wide audience. *The Ring Creek Rip* was turned into a true high-speed rip, the inspiring *Powerhouse Plunge* came into life, the footbridge over Ring Creek Falls was built, as was *Rob's Corners*. *Root 99* and *Lost Loop* were rediscovered, and in an epic of volunteer trail-building, *The Far Side* provided the final crucial link into Crumpit Woods.

Trail development in the spring of 1997, at the time of publication of this book, was busier than ever, with a SORCA proposal to BC Hydro resulting in funding for over ten kilometres of exciting new trails in the Ring Creek North area. Cyclists have become much more pro-active in the maintenance of their trails, and Squamish is starting to discover the fun that lies in their own backyard.

§

First Glance

The Malamute... Short, sharp descents on bedrock from the top of the granite dome in front of the Chief. 1 hour or less.

Squamish Estuary... Flat and open, with easy trails for everyone. Beautiful scenery. 1-1½ hours total riding.

The Smoke Bluffs... Not just rockclimbs! Mostly difficult trails off the summits above Plateau Drive. 2-3 hrs total riding.

Crumpit Woods... One of the best networks of moderate to difficult trails in this guide, adjacent to the Smoke Bluffs. Scenic summits and open deciduous forest. 3-4 hrs total riding.

Ring Creek South... A vast area encompassing the Mamquam River Valley, with many hours of scenic riding on logging roads far beyond the trails described. Home of the *Ring Creek Rip*.

Ring Creek North... North of the Garibaldi Park Road, and extending up into Garibaldi Provincial Park. Strenuous rides of 2-6 hrs mostly moderate and difficult, on a 1000 vertical metre hillside.

Garibaldi Highlands... Mostly long-established trails which link the Alice Lake area with the city streets in the Highlands. 1-3 hours total riding.

Alice Lake... The oldest developed trail system in Squamish, still hugely popular. All grades, especially easy. Good for first-timers and families. 2-4 hours total riding.

Cheekye Fan... The most densely-packed trail network in the Squamish area. Some easy trails, but mostly moderate difficulty. Great family terrain. Watch out for bears. 2-3 hrs total riding.

Cat Lake... One short easy loop, but mostly steep difficult terrain, and one big ride into the alpine. 2-3 hours total riding.

Brohm Lake... An excellent network of moderate trails developed by the Forest Service close to Highway 99. Easy to combine with Alice Lake and Cheekye Fan. 2hrs total riding.

Cheakamus Canyon... One short trials-fest, a burly half-day ride along Evans Ridge, and the classic grind up the Canyon.

Recommended Rides

Squamish Estuary

🟢 Pleasant rides on grassy dikes close to downtown.

The Smoke Bluffs

🟦 ½-1hr. *Summers Eve* and *Endo*.

♦ 1-2hrs. From *Summers Eve*, head up *Mountain of Phlegm* to Smoke Bluff Summit, down *Pipe Trail*, up *Cougar Ridge* and over the hill back to *Summers Eve*.

♦♦ ¾-1½hrs. Up *Mountain of Phlegm*, down *White Bronco,* up *MoP* again, then down *Tree Hugger*. Finish on *Summers Eve*.

Crumpit Woods

🟦 1-2hrs. *The Far Side*, *Root 99* and *S&M Connector*, taking in *Lost Loop* along the way. Either direction.

♦ 1-2 hrs. *Meet Yer Maker* or *Five Point Hill*.

Ring Creek

🟢❤ 2-2½hrs. *The Ring Creek Rip*. Strenuous.

🟦 1-1½hours. Climb up *Ring Creek FSR*, descend *Pseudotsuga* and return via any of the lower roads or trails to the start.

🟦❤ 3-4hours: *Powersmart*. As well as being a great ride on its own, this ride makes a tremendous finale to a day into Elfin Lakes.

🟦❤ 4-6 hours: From Westway Avenue in Valleycliffe, ride through Crumpit Woods, up the Mamquam FSR, down the *Ring Creek Rip*, up Garibaldi Park Road, down *Powersmart*, and back to Crumpit.

♦ 2-3hrs. *The Powerhouse Plunge* to finish *The Ring Creek Rip*.

♦❤ 2-3 hours. Up Ring Creek FSR and down *One Man's Garbage,* then *Another Man's Gold*. Cross Ring Creek and climb the first kilometre of the *Ring Creek Rip*. Turn right and finish down the *Powerhouse Plunge*. For a harder ride (some ♦♦), climb up Garibaldi Park Road and add the *The Nineteenth Hole*, allowing 3-4 hours total time.

Garibaldi Highlands

🟢 1-1½ hours return. *Jacks Trail* or *Mashiter Trail* (either direction) to Alice Lake.

🟦 ½hr. *Roller Coaster*. A great finish to *The Mashiter Trail*.

Recommended Rides

Alice Lake

🟢 1-1½ hours. *Four Lakes Trail North* (when open), *Dead End Connector*, up *Robs Corners*, down the Alice Ridge Road to *Four Lakes Trail South* (when open).

🟦 2-2½ hours. *Four Lakes Trail* or Alice Ridge Road to *Dead End Loop*, up *Rock n' Roll* and down *Ed's Bypass*, *Robs Corners*, *Cliffs Corners*, *Don't Tell Jude* and back via *Tracks From Hell*.

◆ 1-2 hours. Via any trail to *Made In The Shade*.

Cheekye Fan

🟦 1 hour. *Larry's Loop*, best ridden counter-clockwise. Mostly easy terrain. Watch for bears near the dump.

◆ ½ hour. *The Undertaker*.

Cat Lake

🟢 1 hour. From the parking area near Highway 99, ride the *Cat Lake Loop*. Get there via *Here Kitty Kitty* for extra spice.

◆ 1-2 hours. Pedal up Cheekye FSR (the main road) to *Nine Lives*, then back up to ride down *I Am Canadian* and *Hare Scramble*. Finish via *Catwalk* and *Promenade Loop*.

Brohm Lake

🟦 1-1½ hours. The fine combination of *Alder Trail and High Trail*, ridden in a counter-clockwise direction is similar to, but more strenuous than, the *Four Lakes Trail* at Alice Lake. Add *Cheakamus Loop* for a stiffer workout.

Cheakamus Canyon

🟦 ❤️ 2-3 hours. The classic climb up from the Cheakamus River to Highway 99. Scenic, strenuous, unforgettable.

The Test of Metal Course

❤️ ❤️ This famous race course offers a great day out as a recreational ride, covering 65 kilometres of some of the best terrain in Squamish. For a shorter ride, do the northern half back to the Mamquam River or the harder southern section around the *Ring Creek Rip* and Crumpit Woods. Fastest time in 1996 was 2 hours 49 minutes.

SQUAMISH

Facilities

Coffee... Starbucks, in the Squamish Station Mall next to the IGA, offers reliably bold coffee while the Sunflower Bakery and Xanthines, both located on Cleveland, have more of a local feel and delicious baked goods.

Groceries... There are three large grocery stores in the downtown area and one in the Garibaldi Highlands.

Restaurants... Fast-food on every corner as well as many high quality restaurants scattered throughout the district.

Pubs... There are two of special interest: The Howe Sound Inn and Brewing Company on Cleveland Ave, a friendly and lively atmosphere, daily specials, and their own in-house brews served in true 20 oz pints. The Shady Tree Pub, next to Tantalus Bike Shop, is another spot to quench your thirst.

Bank Machines... There are three banks in the downtown core as well as bank machines at the IGA Plus supermarket, Save-On-Foods, the Highlands Mall, and some gas stations.

Showers... The Brennan Park Leisure Center on Loggers Lane offers showers, a hot tub, a sauna, a full size pool, and exercise equipment all for a very reasonable fee. Free showers, although more primitive, can be found in the changing rooms near the playing fields south of the leisure center.

Bike Shops... Two. Corsa Cycles on Cleveland Ave (the main street) in downtown, and Tantalus Bike Shop at 40446 Government Road in Garibaldi Estates: turn west at the intersection of Highway 99 and Garibaldi Way, then right.

Camping... The walk-in campground at the Stawamus Chief for $7.00 per night is convenient, as is the Municipal campground at Brennan Park Leisure Center. Try also the Alice Lake Provincial Park camground.

Local Radio... Canada's national radio station, the CBC, can be picked up at 1260 on your AM dial and 92.1 FM. Commercial radio at 107.1 FM.

Trail Ownership

The following list is intended to give an indication of the land ownership and jurisdiction of the trails in each area. The vast majority of trails in the Squamish area are on public land: crown, municipal, and provincial park. Significant areas however, are owned privately. The trails described which are privately-owned are all on undeveloped land with no habitation or industrial activity, where the public has used the existing trails, in most cases, for many years. Trails believed to be on private land close to residences, industrial plants or otherwise developed commercially, have been excluded.

When out on the trails, it is no easy matter to determine jurisdiction boundaries in the absence of signage. But whether the land be privately-owned or within the public domain, the way in which the trail is used should be the same: with respect. Someone, somewhere, has responsibility to care for it and that job is made easier by minimising erosion, leaving no garbage, respecting other users and observing any posted signage.

The Malamute... Undeveloped private and crown land.

Squamish Estuary... Municipal and undeveloped private.

The Smoke Bluffs... Undeveloped private above Plateau Drive, municipal in the area of the crags.

Crumpit Woods... Mostly undeveloped private with some crown land and municipal land.

Ring Creek South... Crown land.

Ring Creek North... Crown land and BC Parks.

Garibaldi Highlands... Undeveloped private, crown land and municipal land.

Alice Lake... BC Parks and crown land.

Cheekye Fan... Undeveloped private, crown land and municipal land.

Cat Lake... Crown land.

Brohm Lake... Crown land.

Cheakamus Canyon... Crown land, BC Rail.

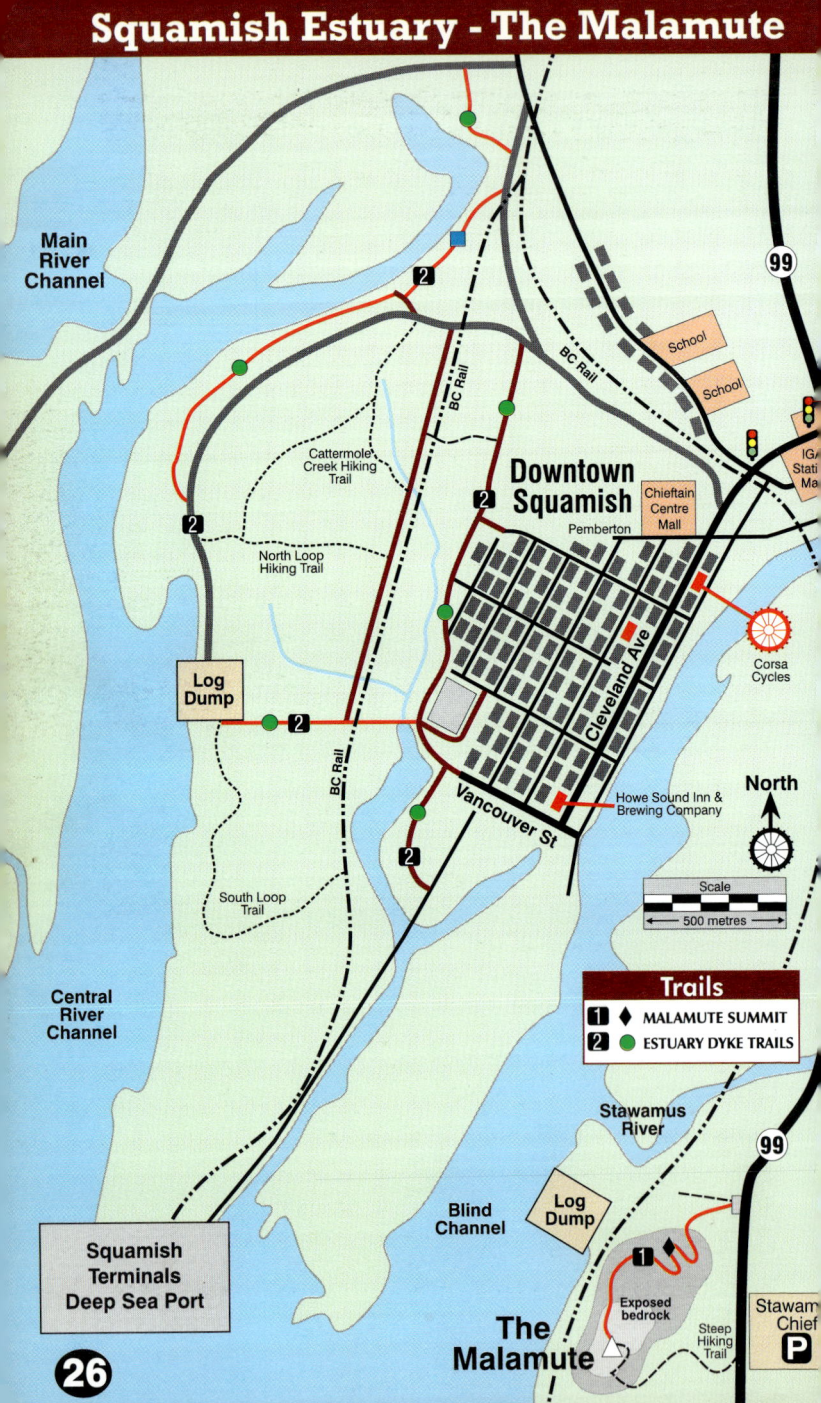

The Malamute

The Malamute is the small rocky hill in front of the Chief on the west side of Highway 99. Well known to climbers for many years, the nonedescript eastern aspect hides a grand sweep of crags on the west side, rising abruptly from the sea for 150 metres to an exposed summit of open bedrock slabs. The views in all directions are sweeping: Squamish and Mt Garibaldi to the north; the Estuary to the west; Shannon Falls and the expanse of Howe Sound to the south; and the humbling mass of the Grand Wall of the Chief to the east.

1   Malamute Summit   ◆
This unique bedrock trail descends from the top of the hill in a northerly direction, joining with the main climber's trail at the Highway, 100m north of the Chief parking lot. A stiff climb with a few hike-a-bikes leads up to the summit slabs in 10mins or less. Descend the way you came or follow another moss-free line. Please stay on established trails to avoid tearing up any vegetation. The best nearby parking is at the Chief.

Squamish Estuary

The Squamish Estuary is a dynamic environment where six glacial rivers pour into the saltwater of the Pacific. Rich in plant and marine life, this magical place is governed by the daily rise and fall of the tides. The glassy sheen of a quiet pool transforms into a dozen gurgling waterways only a few hours later. You can enjoy a different experience with each visit, so take the time to appreciate it—leave your bike behind and follow the hiking trails which lead into the heart of the meadows. Sit down at the edge of the water, tune out the sounds of the city and relax. Remarkably, the estuary has no protection from development and much of the area where the trails exist is threatened by industrial expansion. Park in the downtown area or ride in from elsewhere.

2   Estuary Dykes   ●
This is not a place for hammerheads. The riding in the Estuary is primarily on wide, flat, grassy dykes perfectly suited to an early morning or a lazy late afternoon cruise with the family. The smaller trails branching off these dykes are too boggy, rooty, and tight for cycling, but make fantastic hiking and learning excursions.

The Smoke Bluffs

Trails

- **3** 🟢 STAWAMUS DYKE
- **4** 🟢 CRUMPIT CRK. CRUISE
- **5** 🟢 SMOKE BLUFF TRAIL
- **6** ♦♦ BANZAI PIPELINE
- **7** 🟦 SUMMER'S EVE
- **8** 🟦 ENDO
- **9** ♦ MTN OF PHLEGM
- **10** ♦♦ WHITE BRONCO
- **11** ♦♦ TREE HUGGER
- **12** 🟦 PIPE TRAIL
- **13** ♦ COUGAR RIDGE
- **14** 🟢 THE CHICANES
- **15** 🟢 LEISURE CENTRE

Scale: 400 metres
Contours are approximate at 50m intervals

North

Mamquam River
Gravel Quarry
Private No Entry

Brennan Park Leisure Centre
Showers
Hot Tub
Pool
Parking
Camping

BC Forest Service

Loggers Lane
Loggers Sports Ground
Raven Drive
Finch Drive

Crumpit Woods
Great views
Rough Hiking Trail
See page 32 for more trail info in this area

Quarry Private No Entry

Loggers Lane

Smoke Bluffs Parking Lot

Smoke Bluff Summit

Cougar Ridge
Lake Kudabean

The Smoke Bluffs
Hiking Trails
Rockclimbing

Big Log
Crumpit Creek

Plateau Drive

7-11
McDonalds

IGA Plus Groceries
Starbucks & more

Corsa Cycles
Howe Sound Brew Pub

Blind Channel
Vista Cres

Crumpit Creek
Westway Ave
School
Food Pub

Westway Ave

Stawamus River

Mamquam FSR

The Chief

99
28

The Smoke Bluffs

This suburban playground is well known for a great variety of rock climbing routes on the numerous crags. Less well known are the many fat tire trails largely hidden from view east of, and above the crags. Do NOT park on any of the residential streets near the crags. If you want to park nearby, use the Smoke Bluff Parking Lot or the Leisure Centre, both on Loggers Lane. Most of the higher trails are difficult, reflecting the steep rocky terrain, so be prepared for hike-a-bikes as well as fun. The heavily used Smoke Bluffs Loop trail is not suited to cycling—it is way steep and has numerous stairs.

Riding in this area is naturally combined with the trails in Crumpit Woods immediately to the east. Parking is possible at the top of Westway Ave in Valleycliffe. A wide swath of clearcut (a gas pipeline) is the demarcation line between the two areas.

3 Stawamus River Dyke
A pleasant river-side alternative to the streets of Valleycliffe, despite the occasional gate and piles of boulders which the bike must be carried over.

4 Triple C (Crumpit Creek Cruiser)
Peaceful and pleasant. This short connector trail drops from Plateau Drive to Crumpit Creek behind the Cliffside Pub. It continues to follow the creek to near the junction of Westway Ave and Guildford.

5 Smoke Bluff Trail
This major connector trail is a great short-cut between the Smoke Bluff Parking Lot on Loggers Lane and Plateau Drive in Valleycliffe, skirting below a number of popular rock climbing crags. Use caution, as many hikers, residents and climbers use this trail.

6 Banzai Pipeline ◆
Not for wet weather! Take the Smoke Bluffs Trail up from the Smoke Bluff Parking Lot. Where the trail zigs left into the trees, continue under the powerlines. Look for an inobvious line off to the right heading toward a large black steel pipe. The north (right) side of the pipe is the line of choice on the steep granite slab. The pipe can be seen from Highway 99.

7 Summer's Eve ■
Running roughly parallel to Plateau Drive in Valleycliffe, this pleasant trail links the *Smoke Bluffs Loop Trail* with *Endo*. It is most commonly ridden from the east as an approach to *Mountain Of Phlegm*. Easy at the eastern end, harder toward the west. Expect housing development in this area.

30 THE SMOKE BLUFFS

8   Endo   ■
Short and sweet, this technical trail is best ridden from east to west. A challenging log crossing to warm you up, steep drop-offs, and a smokin' finish makes you wish it were longer. A great trail for sapping that last little bit of energy you may have on the way out of Crumpit Woods.

9   Mountain of Phlegm   ◆
A few hike-a-bike sections, but otherwise an interesting descent or a challenging climb from *Summer's Eve* to the Smoke Bluff Summit. Numerous switchbacks and viewpoints.

10   White Bronco   ◆◆
Talk about getting away with murder! A very steep and challenging plunge down the south side of Smoke Bluff Summit. Unlikely and intimidating rock slabs and tight dirt chutes—all rideable. A short (30 second) hike-a-bike from the finish to exit near the bottom of *Mountain of Phlegm*.

11   Tree Hugger   ◆◆
From the top of Smoke Bluff Summit, steep, awkward slabs with grand views of Howe Sound, a 20 metre teeter along the top of a huge fallen tree (hence the name), a banked corner, another log teeter and more steep slabs lead down to the Smoke Bluffs Loop Trail. At this point, (obvious) turn left and walk downhill for 20 metres to *Summer's Eve* on the left.

12   Pipe Trail   ◆
A highly enjoyable rolling trail which descends from near Smoke Bluff Summit to the high point of the natural gas pipeline bordering Crumpit Woods. Three steep pitches and some tricky riding along a rocky creekbed contribute to its difficulty. It is possible to climb this trail from the Crumpit Woods end, but not recommended.

13   Cougar Ridge   ◆
Enjoy the view! A modest summit overlooking Crumpit Woods which can be accessed from *Summer's Eve* or the *Pipe Trail*. Most enjoyable ridden from north to south, after pedalling up *Mountain of Phlegm* and back down *Pipe Trail*. Expect a few short hike a bikes in either direction, particularly on the steep northern side.

14   The Chicanes   ●
A short series of trails head north-south beneath prominent hydro lines between Raven Drive and the Mamquam River dyke. Many of the chicanes were carved out by moto-cross riders who use this area to play and shred.

15   Leisure Centre Trails   ●
Several short, pleasant trails head south from the Leisure Centre parking lot, passing Loggers Sports ground and exiting on Finch Drive.

Crumpit Woods

Crumpit Woods lie between the Smoke Bluffs and the Ring Creek Lava Flow, bordered by the Mamquam River to the north, and the Powerhouse Bridge Access Road on the south. It is an eclectic area, with several small peaks and ridges offering rolling terrain, and numerous fine viewpoints of the distant peaks. The trails are characterised by moderate difficulty where some technical riding will be found on every ride, as well as some of the most serious descents in this guide. Of the summits, Five Point Hill is the best for biking, with some short hike-a-bikes to the top, then excellent trails descending from the panoramic summit. The Maker hosts one stiff ride from north to south. The most popular moderate ride is through *The Far Side*, *Root 99* and out along the *S&M Connector*, following the route of the Test of Metal race.

The area is popular with a small group of elite motorcycle trials riders who are responsible for developing the trails on Mt Crumpit and some on Five Point Hill. Should you ever have the opportunity to witness them in action, take the time to appreciate their skill. The name of their game is not speed, but control. Trials bikes are surprisingly quiet, nimble and unobtrusive—not to be confused with noisy, trail-shredding moto-cross bikes.

The most convenient parking is on Loggers Lane (as for the Smoke Bluffs) or at the top of Westway Ave. in Valleycliffe.

16   S & M Connector   ■

This gentle trail up Crumpit Creek is the primary southern access into the Crumpit area—a nice introduction to moderate difficulty in the fat tire realm, with only a few rough sections to negotiate and easy access to *Lost Loop*, *Root 99*, *Meet Yer Maker* and *The Far Side*. South of the junction with *Root 99*, there are two successive parallel trails on the west (uphill) side, which can be a better, albeit steeper choice in wet conditions. Take note of the size of the huge stumps left behind from logging in the late 1920's! Although the grade is gentle, the ride back out can be fast.

17   Lacking Head   ◆

This trail climbs from *S&M Connector* to the summit of Mt Crumpit passing the viewpoint of Skull Rock, the exit of *The Raa*, the exit of *Five Point Hill Southside* and the Lacking Head viewpoint along the way. Expect a number of short hike-a-bike sections on the way up, but an exciting ride down.

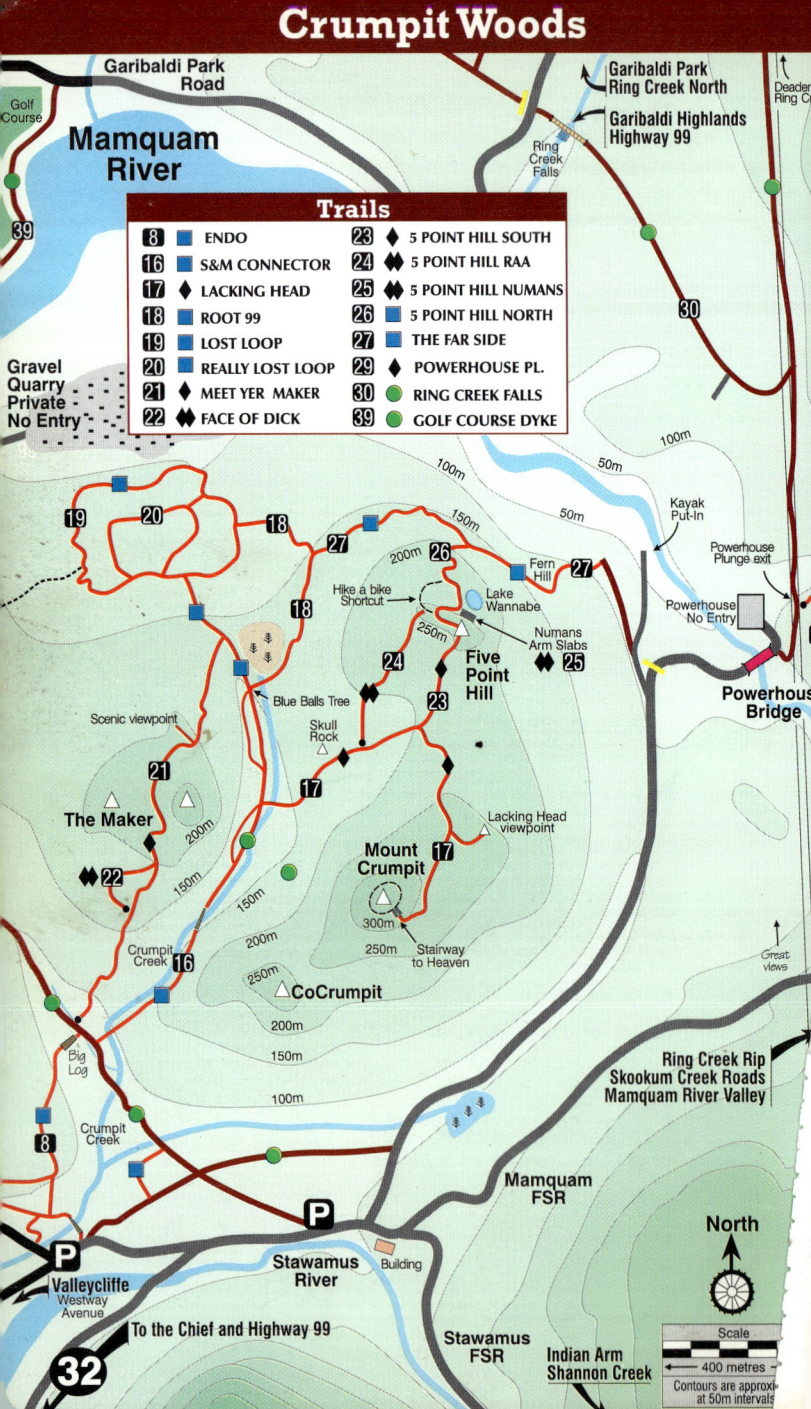

CRUMPIT WOODS 33

18 Root 99 ■
A chunk of the original trail was swallowed by a gravel pit. What remains is a flat, partly-technical trail offering a few moderate obstacles.

19 Lost Loop ■
Obstacle after obstacle, none of which are daunting, is what this sinuous trail is about. While the vertical change is insignificant, the constant mental and physical effort required to successfully clear the obstacles will leave you feeling as though you have just ridden a much longer trail.

20 Really Lost Loop ■
Legend has it that a few lost riders are still hopelessly circling this well named loop within *Lost Loop*. Get out before dark!

21 Meet Yer Maker ◆
A Crumpit Woods classic. This is an excellent ride from *S&M Connector*, up a short but demanding climb with two moderate hike-a-bike sections to the saddle between the twin summits of The Maker, and a spectacular descent riddled with obstacles. Lower your seat and don't stop smiling!!

22 Face of Dick ◆◆
A variation off *Meet Yer Maker*—short and viciously sharp down a series of notorious rock steps. Ouch! Look for a small metal sign on the right.

23 Five Point Hill — Southside ◆
A short, rocky start launches you southward down this fine descent off the summit. After 150 metres the angle eases, then rolls on to *Lacking Head*.

24 Five Point Hill — The Raa ◆◆
A serious, rolling descent from the northern end of Five Point Hill to *Lacking Head*, involving numerous rock steps and painful landings.

25 Five Point Hill — Numan's Arm ◆◆
On the north side of Five Point Hill, just above Lake Wannabe are a trio of short, but intimidating granite slabs. A fine introduction to steep stone.

26 Five Point Hill — Northside ■
This is the northern approach to the summit of Five Point Hill from *The Far Side*. Many very tight corners easily earn this trail the award for most-switchbacks-per-metre. Challenging in either direction.

27 The Far Side ■
An unlikely trail born out of necessity for the 1996 Test of Metal race, it is a result of countless volunteer hours by many people. It traverses the steep northern slope of Crumpit Woods above the Mamquam River, and is a pleasant excursion in either direction, although most often ridden from the eastern end. The open deciduous forest, rare in this area, makes winter riding brighter and more pleasant than one would expect.

SQUAMISH

Ring Creek South – Mamquam River

Nine Mile Bridge
After crossing Nine Mile Bridge, keep left at a major fork, then climb Lava Flow Hill. 150m after the top of the hill, turn left in a clearing to start the Ring Creek Rip.

Skookum Creek
Top of Lava Flow Hill

North

Old logging road continues for several kilometres into upper Ring Creek.

Garibaldi Provincial Park

Ring Creek

Paul Ridge

Garibaldi Park Road

Elfin Lakes

Toyota
Chevy

Spectacular views of Mamquam Mt and the icefields

Raffuse Creek

Scale
1200 metres
Contours are approximate at 100m intervals

Ring Creek Lava Flow
The basalt rock between Ring Creek and the Mamquam River originated from an eruption of Mt Garibaldi, about 8000BC. The lava flowed as far as the north edge of Crumpit Woods.

Hydro Project

Ring Creek North FSR

Mamquam River

The Roll

Trails

8	■	ENDO
16	■	S&M CONNECTOR
18	■	ROOT 99
27	■	THE FAR SIDE
28	●	THE RING CREEK RIP
29	♦	POWERHOUSE PL..
30	●	RING CREEK FALLS TR.
31	♦	ANOTHER MANS GOLD
32	●	RING CK NORTH FSR
33	♦	NINETEENTH HOLE
34	♦	ONE MANS GARBAGE
35	■	POWERSMART
38	●	ELFIN LAKES

See page 37 for more trail info in this area

Ring Creek
Deadend at Ring Creek.

Bonk Hill

Mamquam FSR

Powerhouse Bridge

Indian Arm Shannon Creek

Stawamus FSR

Ring Creek Falls

Mashiter Creek

Thunderbird
Perth Drive

See page 40 for more trail info in this area

Boulevard

Highlands Way South

Mamquam Road

Golf Course

Five Point Hill

Mount Crumpit

See page 32 for more trail info in this area

Gravel Quarry

Crumpit Woods

The Maker

CoCrumpit

Crumpit Creek

Stawamus River

Plateau
Westway

34

Ring Creek South - Mamquam River

Ring Creek South covers an enormous amount of territory between the Mamquam FSR to the south, the *Ring Creek Falls Trail* to the west, Ring Creek to the north, and east as far as the eye can see. This area has only recently been given the attention it deserves with a major overhaul of the *Ring Creek Rip* and construction of the *Powerhouse Plunge*. Many other roads giving long rides branch off the Mamquam FSR, including the Stawamus FSR, which climbs steeply up the Stawamus River, eventually descending to Indian Arm. East of Nine Mile Bridge, there is a lot of worthwhile exploring in scenic mountain terain.

28 The Ring Creek Rip   ●   2-2½hr

This is one of the best trails in this guide, a must-do for all visiting hammerheads down the huge lava flow which erupted from Mt Garibaldi around 8,000BC. Climb up the Mamquam FSR from Crumpit Woods, a steady grind up a well maintained, but steep road for 12 km with superb views of the Mamquam River Canyon and the glaciers of Garibaldi Provincial Park. At the top of Lava Flow Hill, turn left at a clearing to head back west on a rippin' fast big-ring descent down a narrow, winding strip of dirt for 7km (a long abandoned logging road.) A log crossing over Ring Creek gains access to Garibaldi Park Road.

29 Powerhouse Plunge   ◆   2-3hr

Built in the spring of 1996 for the Test of Metal, *"The Plunge"* offers a superb finale to the *Ring Creek Rip*. After 6km of *The Rip*, make a sharp turn to the left. After a kilometre of level singletrack (*The Roll*), steep, technical riding begins abruptly, dropping down to the open, mossy floor of an untouched forest. Then follows a wonderful series of fast, exhilarating switchbacks, unique in this guide, which lead down the final steep slope to exit north of the Powerhouse Bridge. Instead of the scenic grind up the Mamquam FSR, it is possible to reach the trail from the Garibaldi Park Road, by riding up the last kilometre of the *Ring Creek Rip*.

30 Ring Creek Falls Trail   ●

This doubletrack serves as the major link between the trails of Crumpit Woods and the trail networks north of the Garibaldi Park Road. From the north, turn off Garibaldi Park Road about 1km up from the golf course, and head down to the massive and elegant Ring Creek Falls footbridge, built as a cooperative effort between SORCA and local business for the 1996 Test Of Metal. From the south, head north from the Powerhouse Bridge, and after about a kilometre, left at the crest of a hill.

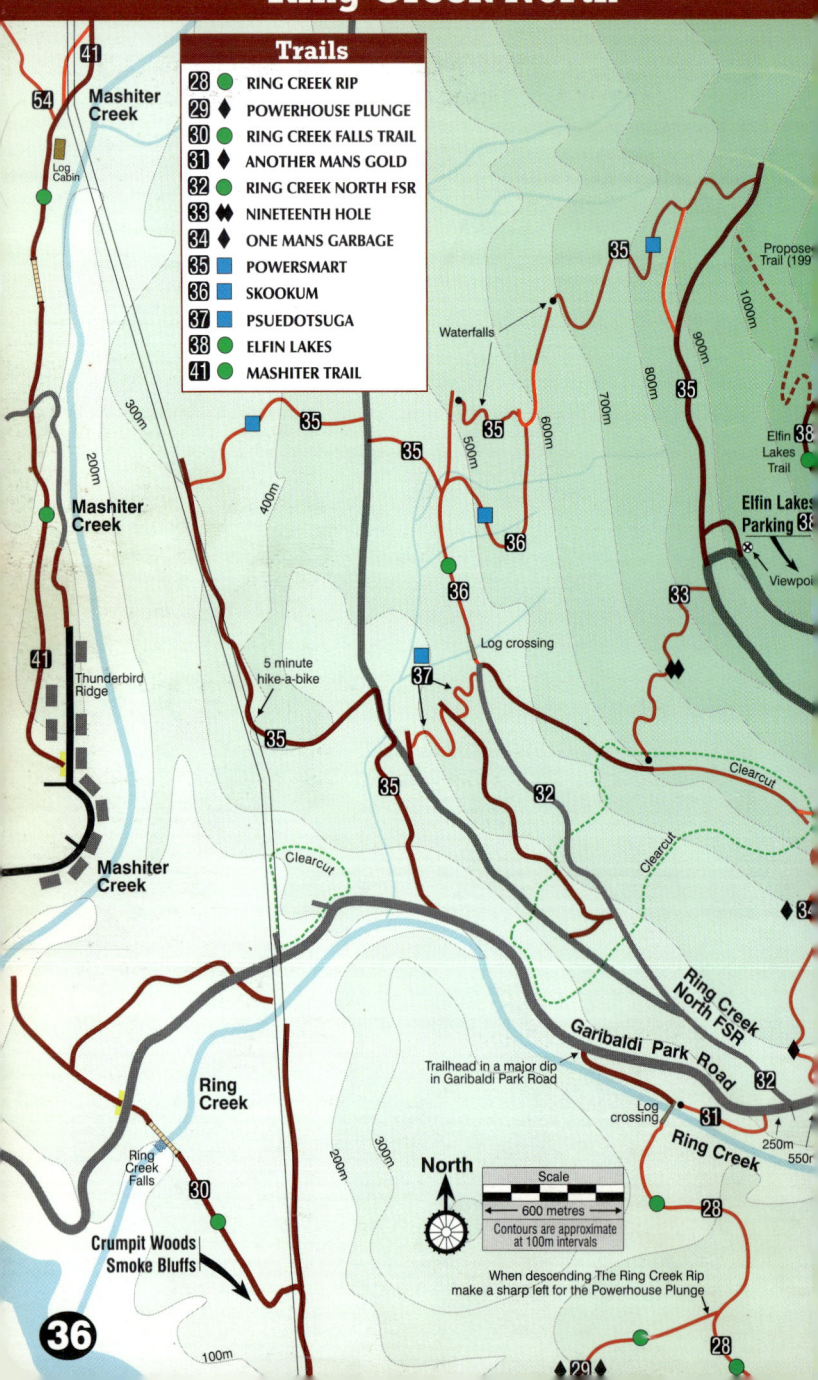

Ring Creek North

Bordered on the east by Garibaldi Provincial Park, by Mashiter Creek to the north and west and by Garibaldi Park Road to the south, this large area boasts a fine network of mostly strenuous trails, accessed from Garibaldi Park Road, often called "the road to Diamond Head," which climbs 15 kilometres from Highway 99 to the Elfin Lakes trailhead. If you choose to ride back down this road, **be very careful of traffic coming up the hill**, as blind corners can make a descent at high-speed a dangerous proposition.

Cyclists share this expanding network of trails with the Small Business Forest Enterprise Program, and as a result, the area is the scene of much forest-related activity. New roads, both permanent and temporary, are appearing on an ongoing basis. Small, selectively logged cutblocks are planned for the coming years and it is possible that trails may be temporarily closed or relocated. Three of the trails listed below (*PowerSmart*, *Skookum*, and *Pseudotsuga*) were made possible through the generous funding of BC Hydro's Youth Employment Initiative Program in cooperation with SORCA and are scheduled for completion in June, 1997. Check with the local bike shops for the most up-to-date information. Convenient parking areas are on the Garibaldi Park Road at the *Ring Creek Falls* trailhead, the Squamish Leisure Centre, or pedal in from Crumpit Woods.

31 Another Man's Gold

This trail drops from the Garibaldi Park road down to the Ring Creek log crossing. Start 200m downhill (west) of the junction with Ring Creek North FSR at a steep drop-off, for a few minutes of trialsy fun. A good short-cut for riders coming off Ring Creek North FSR to the *Powerhouse Plunge*.

32 Ring Creek North FSR

This shady Forest Service Road gives a pleasant climb to access *Psuedotsuga*, *Skookum*, the lower half of *Powersmart*, or *One Man's Garbage*, and offers a fast return to the Garibaldi Park Road from the *Nineteenth Hole* or the upper part of *Powersmart*. Watch out for innocent-looking waterbars which are anything but.

Early on a summer morning, high in the alpine on Paul Ridge on the Elfin Lakes trail — Ron Enns, Carla Fuhre. *Photo: Kevin McLane*

Evening on the Malamute, overlooking Howe Sound. — Brennan Covey. *Photo: Brian Goldstone.*

RING CREEK NORTH 39

33 The Nineteenth Hole   2-2½hr
A trail with a lot of balls. Climb up the Garibaldi Park Road to enjoy over 300 metres of vertical, ear popping fun down a relentlessly steep and technical descent, to be finally spit out into a clearcut with breathtaking views. Choose from several trails to continue back to the base of the hill.

34 One Man's Garbage   1-1½hr
A natural continuation of the *Nineteenth Hole*, but accessible from *Ring Creek North FSR*, this trail traverses east along the top of the clearcut, through a plethora of obstacles before ducking into the woods for more *Nineteenth Hole*-ish fun down to the Garibaldi Park Road.

35 PowerSmart   3-5hr
This tremendous trail drops westward for 750 vertical metres from beyond the top of Garibaldi Park Road—an eclectic and exciting mix of abandoned logging roads, winding singletrack, and BC Hydro right-of-way. It is possible to bail out of the second half of the descent, and head down *Pseudotsuga*, or *Ring Creek North FSR*. Returning down *Powersmart* also makes a superb finale to a long day when returning from the *Elfin Lakes* trail.

36 Skookum
The name is from Chinook jargon, meaning fast, or powerful. This trail truly is. It is an abandoned logging road from the early 40's which has been transformed by sweat and time into a sweeping, smokin' descent from *PowerSmart* to the *Ring Creek FSR* and *Pseudotsuga*. It can also be pedaled uphill to gain the lower half of *PowerSmart* for those lacking the time, energy, or will to grunt to the upper reaches of Garibaldi Park Road.

37 Pseudotsuga (sudo-suga)
A fine twisting trail which snakes downhill through a selectively logged cutblock, giving the shortest loop ride in the area via Ring Creek FSR.

38 Elfin Lakes   5-7hr
See map on page 56. This popular trail into Garibaldi Park offers the best, high alpine easy-to-get-to ride in the Squamish area, to two idyllic little ponds set in stunning meadows east of Mt Garibaldi. Pedal 15km up Garibaldi Park Road to the trailhead, and then by pleasant but continuously steep doubletrack for a further 6km to the top of Paul Ridge, where panoramic alpine views are sure to please even the grumpiest of riders. Another 5km along the crest of the ridge leads to a short descent to the Elfin Lakes shelter, and the end of the trail for mountain bikes, although a number of hiking-only trails continue. Return the way you came *but keep your speed under control* and yield to hikers. A high standard of mountain bike etiquette here may well lead to opening of other areas within Garibaldi Park for biking. The time given allows for a return. However, driving up to the trailhead parking lot to start the ride will cut 2—3 hrs from this time.

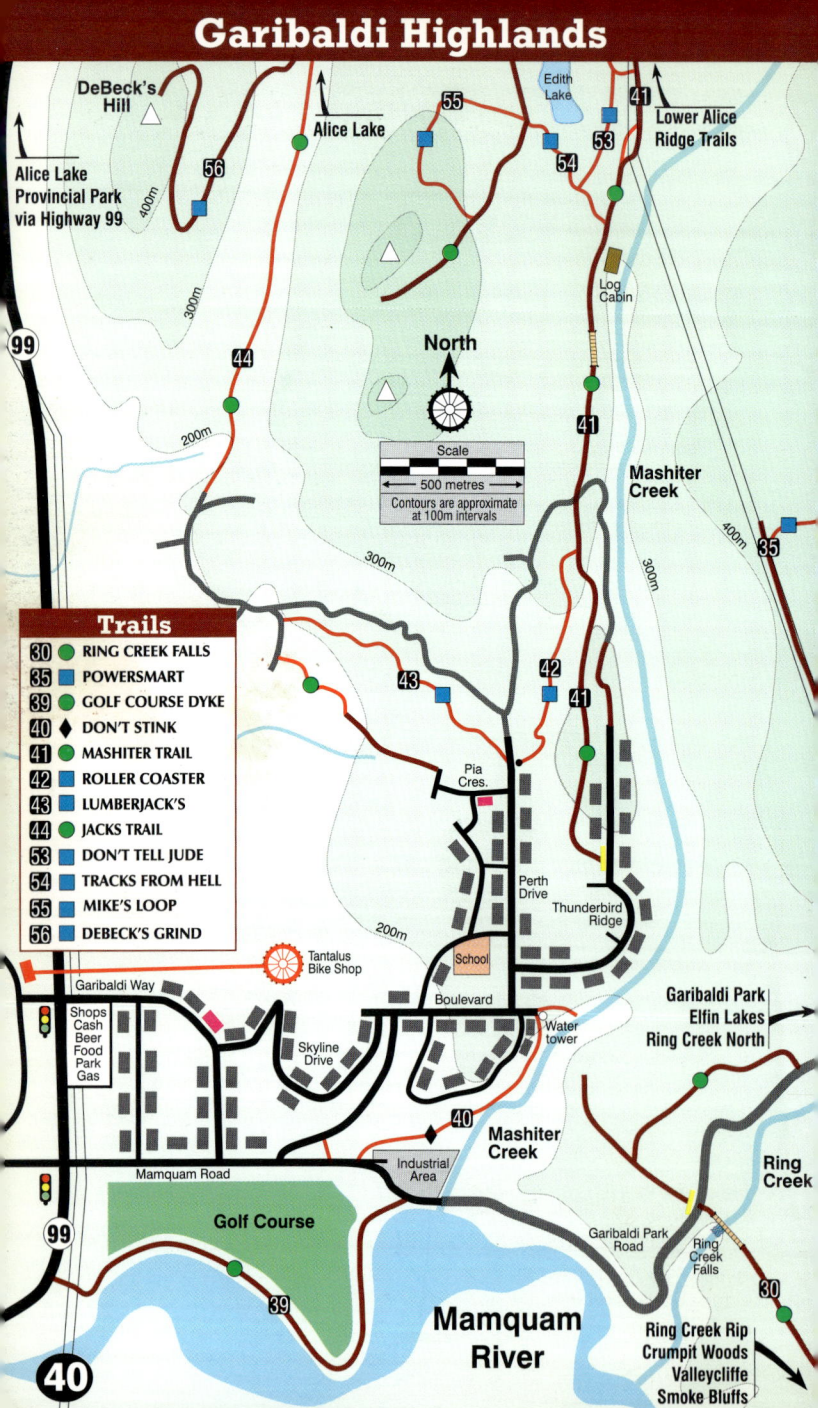

Garibaldi Highlands

North of Garibaldi Highlands, the largest residential area in Squamish, are a number of long-established trails used by local dog walkers, runners, hikers and mountain bikers. Expect moto-crossers too, often seen only as a blur but heard and smelled for hours. South of the Highlands, access to Crumpit Woods is over the footbridge at Ring Creek Falls. East of the Highlands, there are no bridges over Mashiter Creek (yet.) Consequently, *Jack's Trail* and the *Mashiter Trail* see heavy use for travelling to and from the Alice Lake area—much preferred to Highway 99. At the present time, there is considerable new trail development underway, in particular, north of the logging road that joins *Jacks Trail* and the *Mashiter Trail*. Expect many changes here in the next few years.

39 Golf Course Dyke
This is a scenic pathway on a municipal dike around the Golf Course, from Mamquam Road to the Highway. A much better alternative to blacktop.

40 Don't Stink
This steep singletrack starts at the top of the Boulevard and plunges down the side of Mashiter Creek behind Kintyre Drive to Mamquam Road.

41 Mashiter Trail
A wide and friendly trail which climbs gently to connect the Highlands and the lower Alice Ridge area. Suitable for riders of all abilities in either direction. Delightfully fast as a descent. Watch out for hikers!

42 Roller Coaster
Start from the *Mashiter Trail* on a winding path through a clearcut and end with one of the fastest, sweetest, most awe-inspiring hardpack singletrack descents in Squamish. A fine, but all too short example of what singletrack is all about.

43 Lumberjack's Trail
Jack reincarnate. This trail replaced the southern half of *Jack's Trail*, eliminated by logging in 1995. Then it was logged again in 1997. No one can bring good old Jack back.

44 Jack's Trail
Originally, this trail cut a brilliant path between between Alice Lake and Perth Drive in the Garibaldi Highlands. Unfortunately, half of the trail was chewed up by logging, swallowed by a clear-cut, and spit out in the form of a logging road. The northern section that remains is nonetheless a beautiful, gently sloped trail, that is a pleasure to ride in either direction.

Alice Lake

Possible crossing of the Cheekye to Cat Lake trails. You'll either get wet feet, a wet ass, or drown, depending on conditions.

Cheekye River

FOUR LAKES TRAIL NORTH
Closed May 1st to September 15th

Stump Lake

BC Parks Office

Yellow Gate

To Highway 99

Mini Tracks From Hell

to Alice Ridge

Third waterbar after yellow gate

Fawn Lake

Alice Ridge Road

Alice Lake Provincial Park

Cyclists bulletin board & shelter

Yellow gate

North

Alice Lake

DeBeck's Hill

FOUR LAKES TRAIL SOUTH
Closed May 1st to September 15th

Edith Lake

Scale
400 metres
Contours are approximate at 50m intervals

Alice Lake Provincial Park

Tracks

Of Mice and Men Hill

42 To Garibaldi Highlands

Trails

- 41 MASHITER TRAIL
- 44 JACK'S TRAIL
- 45 FOUR LAKES TRAIL
- 46 DEAD END CONN.
- 47 DEAD END LOOP
- 48 ROCK N' ROLL
- 49 ROBS CORNERS
- 50 ED'S BYPASS
- 51 MADE IN THE SHADE
- 52 CLIFFS CORNERS
- 53 DON'T TELL JUDE
- 54 TRACKS FROM HELL
- 55 MIKE'S LOOP
- 56 DEBECK'S GRIND

Alice Lake Area

For years, the only place to go for a decent ride in Squamish was Alice Lake Provincial Park, and the showcase *Four Lakes Trail* still draws in the crowds, although there is now a seasonal closure to mountain bikes during the busy summer months (May 1st to September 15th) to avoid user conflict and excessive trail erosion. This only affects the northern section from Stump Lake to Fawn Lake, and the southern section from Edith Lake to Alice Lake. None of the trails outside the Park boundary are affected. This includes a number of Squamish classics which can be ridden year round, dependent only on the occasional snow cover.

There are rides for everyone, from white knuckle descents and tooth rattling rail grades to gently sloped twisting single track through immature forest. Alice Lake, although often quite crowded, is an excellent place to take a refreshing dip after a hot day's ride.

45 The Four Lakes Trail ●

One of the most popular trails in Squamish, it connects (appropriately) four small lakes: Stump, Fawn, Edith, Alice. It is usually ridden clockwise to take advantage of the gentler climb in that direction. Please remember, the *Four Lakes Trail* is closed to mountain bikes from May 1st to September 15th.

46 Dead End Connector ●

This is the wide trail which connects Edith Lake to the base of *Rock n' Roll* and *Dead End Loop*. Pleasant going north, fast heading south.

47 Dead End Loop ■

Good either way, but most commonly ridden counter-clockwise. It starts at *Rock n' Roll* with an imperceptible climb along an old rail grade, but quickly changes character as it turns west near the Cheekye River. Tight turns, roots, and a few small logs challenge your bike handling ability without threatening your health. A short climb back to the south under the hydro lines brings you to where you started. A short-cut across the loop is possible along the "Mini Tracks From Hell".

48 Rock n' Roll ◆

This is a delightfully steep short hill (some would say brutal) which links the lower trails by the Cheekye River with the *Corners* and trails to the south. It presents either a hike-a-bike up or a challenging surf down. It is a quick way to gain elevation, and sees a lot of traffic due to its strategic location.

Made in the Shade — Mike Carney.
Photo: Bonny Makarewicz

Cougar Ridge — Armand Hurford.
Photo: Brian Goldstone

The Ring Creek log bridge—Kevin McLane
Photo: Rob Cocquyt

VW fun on *My Trail* — Genevieve Leger
Photo: Rob Cocquyt

ALICE LAKE **45**

49 Rob's Corners
A short, but better alternative to the parallel hydro road, *Rob's Corners*, very similar to *Cliff's Corners*, weaves its way through continuous tight turns and rolling terrain north of the Alice Ridge Road.

50 Ed's Bypass
A moderate descent option which turns left off *Made In The Shade* before the real difficulties begin on that trail, exiting onto the hydro line road *(Mashiter Trail)* near the top of *Rock n' Roll*. Obstacle fun.

51 Made in the Shade ♦
Awesome. Serious. Fun. Riders see this trail in many different lights. Those who have ridden it and finished unscathed are sure to like it. Those who have crashed, burned or rolled are likely to share a love-hate relationship with this much-ridden classic.

52 Cliff's Corners
Heading south from the Alice Ridge Road to the *Mashiter Trail*, this short trail is deservedly popular. Banked corners and loose soil dictate a light finger on the front brake. Like *Rob's Corners*, it is most popular as a descent, but beware, as the crash-likelyhood varies directly with the speed at which this trail is ridden.

53 Don't Tell Jude
Don't tell anyone else either. This trail is a bushwack.

54 Tracks From Hell
Make sure that your tires are well pumped up, all screws are tight, and that you have no loose fillings in your mouth, because the centrepiece of this trail offers what may be the hardest level terrain you are ever likely to ride—a rite-of-passage for those new to the area. The "tracks" are actually logging railroad ties from the 1930's. If you survive the shaking, you should manage to stay dry on the long (and so narrow!) boardwalk over a bike-swallowing swamp. For some reason, kids love it.

55 Mike's Loop
Possible in either direction, but best clockwise, begin with a lung searing climb up the aptly named *Of Mice And Men* hill (difficult when descended.) A right turn at the crest will bring you onto a fast twisting single track descent. Continuing straight ahead for a further ten minutes leads to a pleasant lookout and lunch spot.

56 DeBeck's Grind
A stiff and unrelenting climb up an old road leads to the top of this hill and an unusual viewpoint of the Squamish valley. Check your watch when you start and when you eventually arrive at the top, consider that this hill has been climbed in less than 15 minutes by two well-known Squamish brothers trying to smoke each other into the dirt.

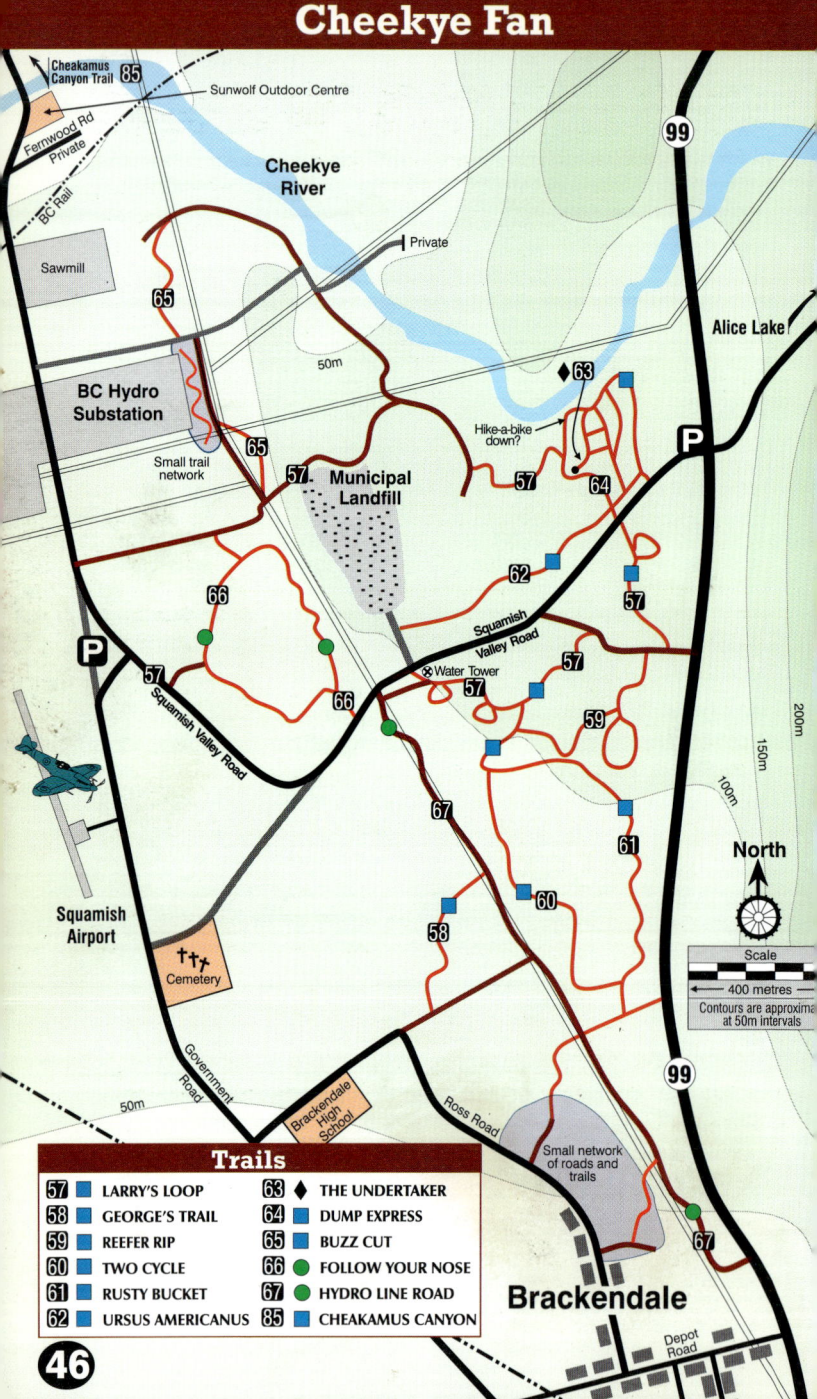

47

Cheekye Fan

Riders who have little mountain biking experience but who wish to improve their technical skills without worrying about splittin' their noggin' would enjoy riding the trails north of Brackendale in the Cheekye Fan. Meandering like rivers, they are generally flat, soft, and riddled with small log pyramids. The atmosphere is unique: one minute you're surrounded by huge cedars and enveloped in darkness-the next you are in a sunny open field with beautiful views of the surrounding mountains. On trails near the Municipal Landfill, keep a sharp lookout for bears.

57 Larry's Loop ■   1hr
By far the most popular loop in the area, this is a gentle smorgasbord of fat tire terrain. Small log pyramids, tight singletrack, abandoned roads, and plenty of options make *Larry's Loop* an excellent starting point.

58 George's Trail 59 Reefer Rip 60 Two Cycle 61 Rusty Bucket ■
All the above are synonyms for quality Cheekye singletrack. Meandering earthen trails through a beautiful forest with a floor carpeted in fluorescent moss. A hearty selection of well built obstacles and variations to satisfy the needs of riders of all abilities.

62 Ursus Americanus ■
One of the most likely spots to encounter a bear in Squamish (close to the dump), this enjoyable singletrack is conveniently fast and tight.

63 The Undertaker
Every area has to have its own no nonsense, what's-the-quickest-way-down-this-hill-even-if-it-means-sliding-down-on-my-face trail. *The Undertaker* takes the steepest way down one of the only hills in the Fan.

64 Dump Express ■
Part of *Larry's Loop,* crossing *Ursus Americanus*.

65 The Buzz Cut ■
A number of roads and short singletrack sections criss-cross the substation clearcut. Together they form *The Buzz Cut*.

66 Follow Your Nose ●
A pleasant obstacle-free loop around a recently pruned woodlot, perfect for hammerheads just cutting their teeth.

67 Hydro Line Road ●
This road runs the entire length of the fan, interrupted only by a short section west of the landfill. Open, rocky, dusty or muddy depending on the weather.

SQUAMISH

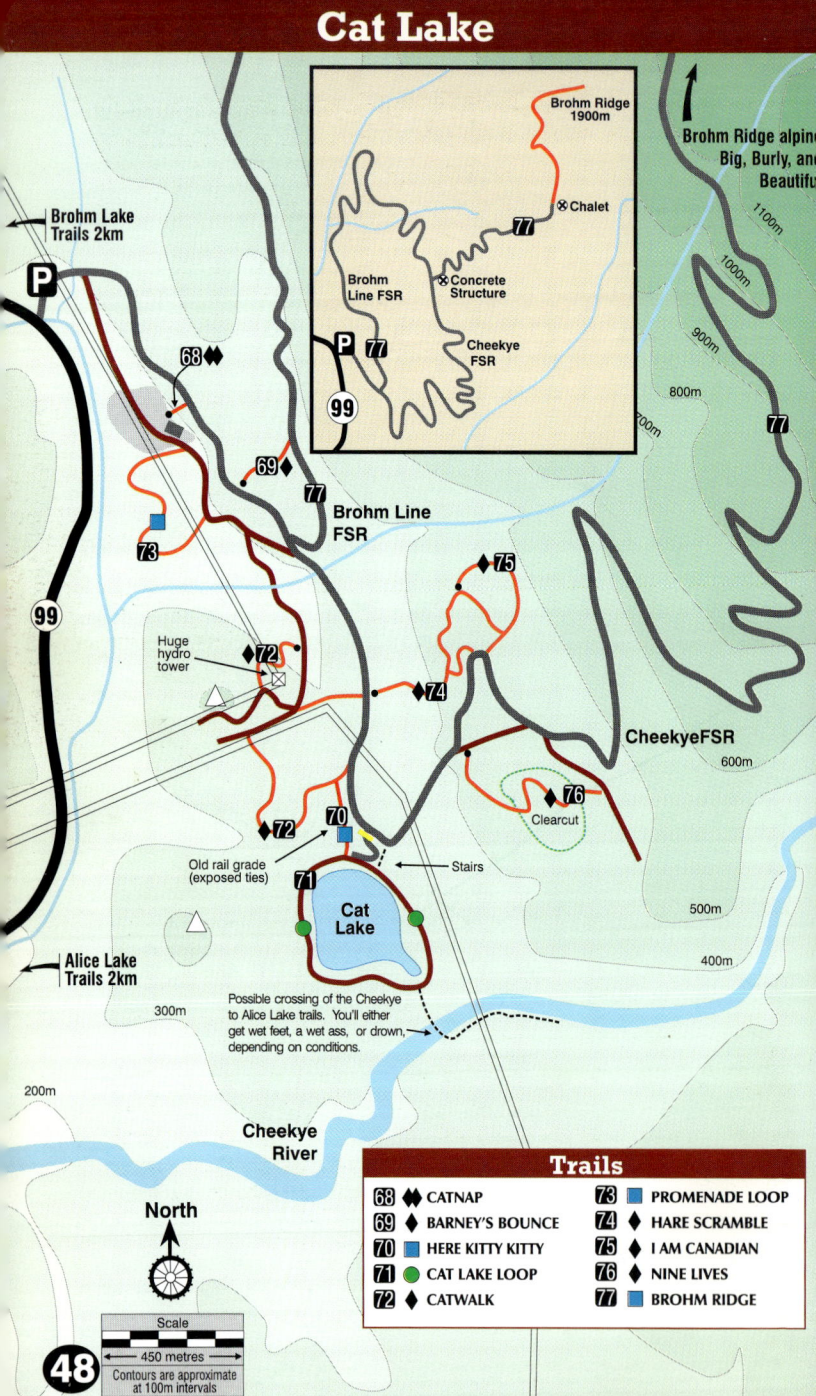

Cat Lake

North of Alice Lake Provincial Park and close to Highway 99, this is an area which boasts short, consistently difficult technical trails, with one notable exception. Steep logging road climbs and rutted, rooty descents are the order of the day. The single exception, a sheep among the wolves, is the Cat Lake Loop, which offers a pleasant spin through the woods around the lake. Rides here can easily be combined with outings nearby in the Alice Lake and Brohm Lake areas. Cat Lake is another great place to go for a swim although it is often crowded, particularly on weekends.

Choose your parking spot carefully, making sure not to block the road, as logging trucks can hammer by at any time. Parking just off Highway 99 is the best choice.

For the brave, it is possible to connect the Cat Lake trails with *Dead End Loop* and the Alice Lake Trails by fording the Cheekye River when the water level is low in the summer.

68 Catnap ◆◆
The quickest way from point A to point B. The drop-in is a doozy.

69 Barney's Bounce ◆
A short, rocky, technical descent off Brohm Line FSR where it levels out after a few minutes of climbing. Rarely ridden.

70 Here Kitty Kitty ■
A friendly descent to Cat Lake. Be sure to take the left fork to follow the old rail grade.

71 Cat Lake Loop ●
A pleasant ride around a beautiful lake. At the southeastern end of the lake a lookout provides views of the Cheekye River.

72 Catwalk ◆
Begin with *Here, Kitty Kitty*, but take the right fork when the rail grade is first encountered. Tight technical singletrack followed by a loose rocky road and back into steep singletrack. A fine mix. A right turn at the junction at the bottom of the steep hill will bring you back to the hydro access road and avoids an ugly and often boggy exit.

73 Promenade Loop ■
An easy spin, usually ridden clockwise on the way back out from the hard riding.

Loonie race action in Squamish
—Scott Ross running (try it!) up *Rock n' Roll*, chased a minute later by his bro Al (inset).
Photos: Rob Cocquyt.

CAT LAKE

74 Hare Scramble ◆
A steep technical descent typical of Cat Lake—used and abused, rutted and ugly. And oh so much fun! While only one line is shown on the map, there are a number of options to choose from along the way.

75 I am Canadian ◆
The Cat Lake Sampler. Hike-a-bikes, creek crossings, roots, steep descents, technical climbs and rutted singletrack all in easy to swallow bite-size portions.

76 Nine Lives ◆
Two minutes of easy climbing off Cheekye FSR, a two minute hardpack descent, two minutes of loose, sandy, rocky hell through an old clear-cut, two minutes of rolling mediocrity and a two minute gentle climb back to where you started. (Times may vary by two minutes.)

77 Brohm Ridge Alpine Loop ●   3-7hr
Offering one of the steepest and most sustained long climbs around Squamish, this fine loop can be ridden in either direction—clockwise is best. Starting from Highway 99 at the Cat Lake entrance, climb up Brohm Line FSR for about 5-6km to a right turn which starts you back southward. A ski and mountain resort is proposed north of this area which offers tantalising opportunites for future trails. Continue south to a junction with the Cheekye FSR and head back down to Cat Lake for the shortest loop.

If you want a really big day into the high alpine, continue climbing steeply on Cheekye FSR through old clearcuts for another hour or so to a private chalet. The road continues north onto Brohm Ridge proper, eventually petering out into the high alpine at about 1900m elevation, on a faint trail more suitable for hiking. From this point, it is a l-o-n-g way back down. Stunning, close up views of Dalton Dome, Atwell Peak, the Table, Alice Ridge and the Squamish valley far below make this a worthwhile trip for lovers of steep, burly climbs.

People will ride the trails long after you have passed by for the last time. Leave a legacy of care and respect. Good karma.

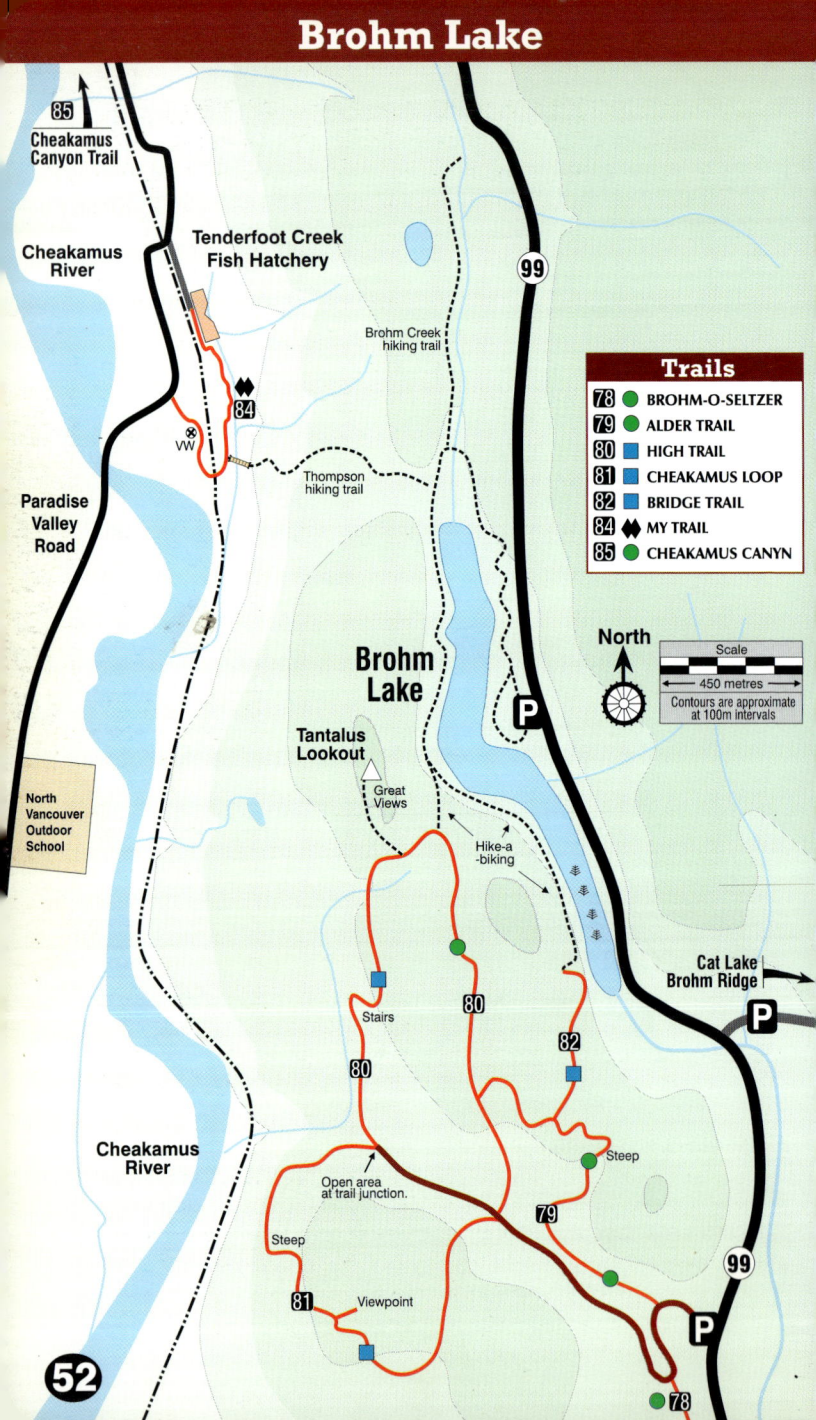

Brohm Lake Interpretive Forest

A network of trails has been built by the Squamish District of the BC Forest Service in the Brohm Lake Interpretive Forest—so you can expect well built, well maintained trails with no obstacles except the occasional steep grade. Only ride the trails that are designated "multi-use" and give hikers a wide berth. Stop and read the interpretive signs to make the most of a fun and educational ride. Trails in this area are easily combined with Cat Lake, Alice Lake, and the Cheekye Fan. The most popular loop, similar to, but more strenuous than the *Four Lakes Trail* at Alice Lake, is *Alder Trail*, *High Trail*, and *Cheakamus Loop*, ridden in a counter-clockwise direction.

The best parking area is not the big public lot on Highway 99 near the lake, the trails which lead from there are not suitable for bikes. Park further south at a smaller lot, south of the Cat Lake access road.

78 Brohm-O-Selter
Abandoned forestry roads connect the Brohm Lake Interpretive Forest with Highway 99 north of the bridge over the Cheekye River. Ridden in either direction, it is an alternative to the noise of the highway.

79 Alder Trail
Who says the Forest Service can't build fun trails? A steep climb up and a magic carpet ride back down the other side.

80 High Trail
Fast. Watch for the stairs.

81 Cheakamus Loop
This trail has two faces. Ridden from counter-clockwise, the steep climb involves a few hike-a-bike sections and some technical spots. The descent, however, is fast, furious, and trouble free. Ridden clockwise, it is a steady and manageable climb followed by an occasionally technical downhill. Good fun no matter how you look at it. Watch out for hikers.

82 Bridge Trail
From *High Trail* to Brohm Lake this trail is a blast. Fast winding and smooth with lots of opportunities for big air. Then, all of a sudden, the air is let out of your sails. The remainder of the trail skirting the lake is rooty, muddy, and rocky. Annoying actually, but maybe it will change. Either spin back up or push your bike to the Connector Trail, another obvious hike-a-bike but a functional means to regain your lost elevation.

Cheakamus Canyon

Cloudburst Mountain

Trail joins Highway 99 approximately 5½km north of Culliton Creek 3½km south of Chance Creek FSR

Awesome views into the canyon

Conroy Creek FSR

Chek rockclimbing area.

Starvation Lake

Trail entrance is opposite small commercial development

Some hike-a-biking

Pilchuck Creek

Upper Squamish Elaho River roads Ashlu Creek roads Stoltman Wilderness

Culliton Creek (Big Orange bridge)

Island Lake

Badly eroded trail. Wet and rocky.

Hut Lake

Rough, rocky double track to Hut Lake. Some hike-a-bike.

Cheakamus River

Swift Creek FSR

North

Scale — 2000 metres
Contours are approximate at 200m intervals

Levette Lake

Private road. No Entry.

This could be the steepest paved road you'll ever ride.

Tenderfoot Creek Fish Hatchery

Brohm Lake

See page 53 for more trail info in this area

Private. No Entry. Evans Lake Forestry Centre

Squamish River

Squamish Valley Road

Cheekye River

Cat Lake

See page 49 for more trail info in this area

54

Tantalus Range

Lake Lovelywater

Stum Lake

P

Squamish

Alice Lake

See page 43 for more trail info in this area

Trails

78	●	BROHM-O-SELTZER
83	■	EVANS RIDGE
84	♦	MY TRAIL
85	●	CHEAKAMUS CANYON
86	■	STARVATION PLUNGE

Cheakamus Canyon

Development of trails in the Cheakamus Valley has been stunted by the unforgiving topography of the area. Trails here tend to follow long abandoned logging roads or old pack trails in the gaps between the rocks. While these trails are somewhat out of the way from downtown Squamish, the charming atmosphere in Paradise Valley and scenic rides make it well worth the effort.

It goes without saying that anyone wishing to ride from Squamish to Whistler should avoid riding Highway 99 and take the beautiful Cheakamus Canyon Trail instead, a famous rocky track which originated at the turn of the century, and is one of the highlights in the Cheakamus Challenge cross-country race each fall.

83 Evans Ridge   3-4hrs
Begin with what must be the steepest paved hill in the corridor to Evans Lake. From here to Levette Lake the road turns to gravel and climbs at a moderate grade. From Levette to Hut Lake the road degrades into loose baby head boulders with steep climbs and short descents. From Hut to Island Lake the road is hardly a road at all. Years of erosion have transformed much of it into a sizable creek, but still somewhat ridable for those searching for an epic out-and-back ride.

84 My Trail ◆◆
A short trials-fest not to be missed, near the Tenderfoot Creek Fish Hatchery. Beautifully constructed obstacles of various degrees of difficulty in an idyllic setting next to Tenderfoot Creek. The coup-de-grace is a challenging ride over a VW Bug. The area is very popular with wintering bald eagles which feast on dead salmon from November to February.

85 Cheakamus Canyon Trail   2-3hrs
Despite being a great descent, this trail is almost always ridden uphill from Paradise Valley to Highway 99. Perhaps this is due to the annual Cheakamus Challenge race which attracts over a thousand riders who eagerly await the chance to fight gravity up this famous trail.

86 Starvation Lake Plunge ■
This little-known link exists from Highway 99 down to Starvation Lake on the Cheakamus Canyon Trail. Turn west onto a wide but not-obvious trail immediately opposite a small industrial development on the Highway, just south of Conroy Creek FSR. A short climb leads on to a rocky descent down an old road, steep in places, to the lake.

Brandywine to Function Junction

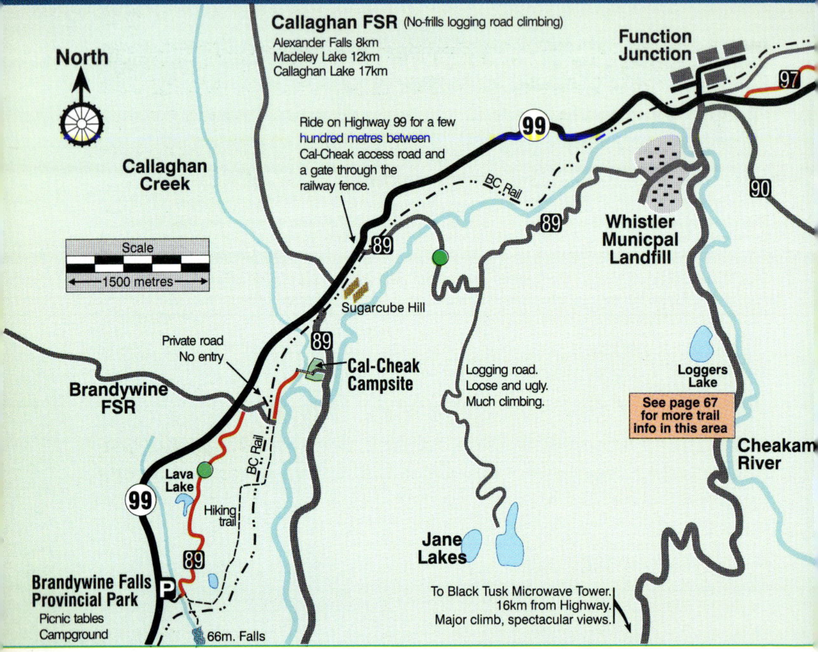

North

Callaghan FSR (No-frills logging road climbing)
Alexander Falls 8km
Madeley Lake 12km
Callaghan Lake 17km

Function Junction

Ride on Highway 99 for a few hundred metres between Cal-Cheak access road and a gate through the railway fence.

Callaghan Creek

Scale — 1500 metres

Sugarcube Hill

Private road No entry

Brandywine FSR

Cal-Cheak Campsite

Logging road. Loose and ugly. Much climbing.

Whistler Municpal Landfill

See page 67 for more trail info in this area

Loggers Lake

Cheakamus River

Lava Lake

Hiking trail

Brandywine Falls Provincial Park
Picnic tables
Campground

66m. Falls

Jane Lakes

To Black Tusk Microwave Tower. 16km from Highway. Major climb, spectacular views.

Lucille Lake - Pinecrest

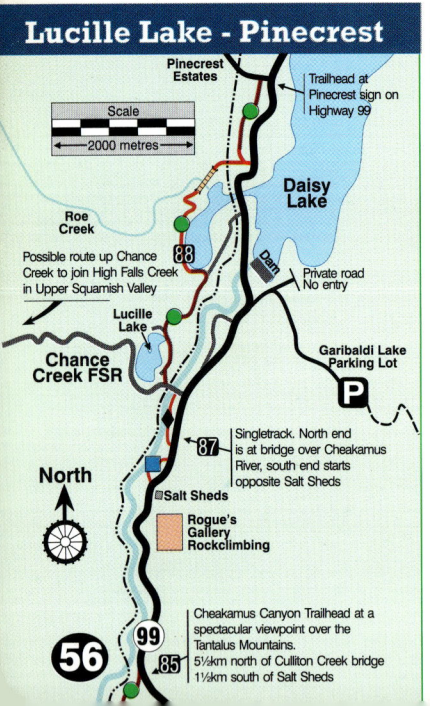

Pinecrest Estates
Trailhead at Pinecrest sign on Highway 99

Scale — 2000 metres

Daisy Lake

Roe Creek

Possible route up Chance Creek to join High Falls Creek in Upper Squamish Valley

Private road No entry

Lucille Lake

Chance Creek FSR

Garibaldi Lake Parking Lot

Singletrack. North end is at bridge over Cheakamus River, south end starts opposite Salt Sheds

Salt Sheds

Rogue's Gallery Rockclimbing

North

Cheakamus Canyon Trailhead at a spectacular viewpoint over the Tantalus Mountains.
5½km north of Culliton Creek bridge
1½km south of Salt Sheds

Elfin Lakes

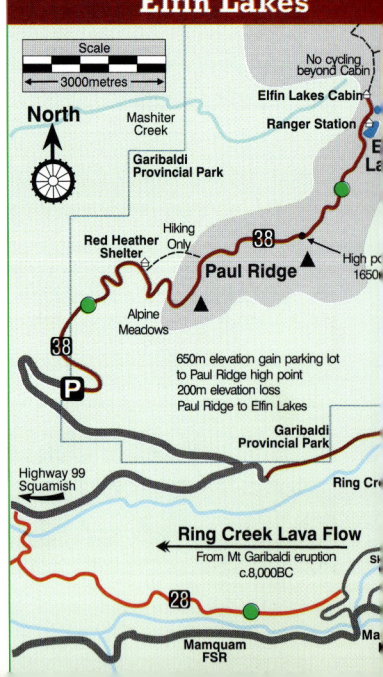

No cycling beyond Cabin
Elfin Lakes Cabin
Ranger Station

Scale — 3000 metres

North

Mashiter Creek

Garibaldi Provincial Park

Hiking Only

Red Heather Shelter

Paul Ridge

High pt 1650

Alpine Meadows

650m elevation gain parking lot to Paul Ridge high point
200m elevation loss Paul Ridge to Elfin Lakes

Garibaldi Provincial Park

Highway 99 Squamish

Ring Cr

Ring Creek Lava Flow
From Mt Garibaldi eruption c.8,000BC

Mamquam FSR

Chance Creek - Function Junction

Highway 99 follows a natural corridor north of the Cheakamus Canyon, and the following trails on the east and west sides are excellent alternatives to the blacktop. After climbing up the Canyon, the Cheakamus Challenge race follows these trails to Function Junction, at which point it climbs up over *Microwave Hill* and *Northwest Passage* to the finish in Whistler Village. Riding the race course is a popular (but long) day out, best achieved by starting from the Alice Lake Provincial Park turn-off on Highway 99.

87 The Doris Burma Memorial Trail ◆

This short, funky trail north of the Cheakamus Canyon, best ridden north to south, runs parallel to Highway 99 between the Salt Sheds and Chance Creek FSR. It offers a diversion from the blacktop, but is hard going and demands skill to enjoy. Built for the 1996 Cheakamus Challenge.

88 Chance Creek - Pinecrest

A good excursion well worth the effort, away from the Highway around the west side of the Daisy Lake dam. Lots of variety from singletrack to open gravel roads, following the course of the Cheakamus Challenge race. Turn off the Highway at Chance Creek FSR, cross the Cheakamus River, keep right and follow roads and trails northward, emerging back onto the Highway near the Pinecrest subdivison.

89 Brandywine - Function Junction   2-3hr

This is a classic ride on trails and gravel roads east of Highway 99 between Brandywine Falls Provincial Park and Function Junction. Although it is good in either direction, north to south is easier as less climbing is required. Starting from the Park, take a sharp left turn after crossing the footbridge over Brandywine Creek at the back of the parking lots. Rolling bedrock (an old lava flow) leads to a right turn at a gravel road. After a few hundred metres (keep right at a Private Entrance sign), cross the railway tracks, and go sharp left onto sweet singletrack along the south bank of Callaghan Creek. Cross the creek on a huge suspension bridge (don't jam your wheel between the boards!), through the campground which follows, and along the road back to Highway 99. Ride up the highway for a few hundred metres until possible to cross the railway at a gate through the fence. An old road drops northward to the Cheakamus River, then begins to climb steeply for 10-15 minutes. More up and down, fast and fun, leads to the Whistler Municipal dump (bears everywhere), blacktop and Function Junction. The fastest riders in the Cheakamus Challenge will cover this entire section in less than 35 minutes! Return along the highway.

WHISTLER

The Resort Municipality of Whistler has earned a well-deserved reputation as one of the world's great winter ski resorts. However, the many attractions of the warmer half of the year, of which the mountainbike is a major one, now rival winter activity and Whistler can claim with ease to be a four season resort on par with the world's best.

As with most aspects of life in Whistler, the shape of the narrow mountain valley along which the Municipality is stretched has determined the character of mountainbike trails. On the valley floor, difficulty rarely exceeds a moderate level, whereas on the valley sides, particularly the west side, trails are steep and rugged, offering major workouts, fine scenery and thrilling descents. The two ski mountains, Whistler and Blackcomb, also have numerous trails: around the base in the latter case, and up on the hill on a user-pay basis at Whistler.

Over a period of many years, considerable effort has gone into development of a major community trail system on the generally flat valley floor: the Valley Trail. Today, this civic gem sees heavy usage far beyond the original expectations, from commuters and tourists, runners, rollerbladers, and mountainbikers travelling from one location to another.

The riding season usually runs from April to October, although in a heavy snow year such as 96-97, snow can linger on the higher trails such as *Binty's* well into June. The first trails to be snow-free are usually in the Village—Lost Lake area, and as with Squamish, expect lots of mud at that time of the year. Summer heat can be a bit much for some people, although others just can't get enough of it.

Whistler regularly hosts major mountainbike races, such as BC Cup and Canada Cup events, and the Cactus Cup. Locally, however, there is a very active weekly race calendar organised by the Whistler Off Road Cycling Association (WORCA) and local bike shops. Mass starts of over 100 riders are now commonplace.

It is not difficult to see why Whistler has become so successful as a mountainbike destination: a great variety of trails that have something to suit every taste—family outings on easy trails, long rides, hard descents, alpine rides, valley floor rides, and several highly developed networks of technical trails—most within a reasonable pedalling distance of the Village and the amenities which have made Whistler famous.

The Whistler Off-Road Cycling Association, commonly known as WORCA, was formed in 1989 by Bob Eakins, Paul Rawlinson, Richard Kelly, Vincent Massey, Charlie Doyle and Eric Wight. The intent at the time was to lobby against pending closure of trails in Garibaldi Provincial Park, occasioned by the 1990 Master Plan. As a result of their effort, the Cheakamus Lake and Elfin Lakes trails remained open for cyclists' use. In the years that followed, continued growth in the sport, education in trail awareness and maintenance, and creation of the infamous "Loonie Race" helped membership expand to 160 members in 1996.

In recent years, the popularity of Whistler trails, particularly the harder ones, has led to significant erosion problems, foreshadowing the need to manage and plan. In this respect, WORCA is taking a pro-active role with several levels of government to help manage the growing popularity of mountainbiking: working cooperatively with government and users to rebuild trails as needed; to establish new trails where they are strategically beneficial; and providing a solid social structure for the sport in the Whistler Valley.

———— § ————

First Glance

Upper Cheakamus Valley... A large area of generally strenuous rides south of Whistler which extends to the edge of Garibaldi Park. Encompasses the Whistler Interpretive Forest trails, and the *Microwave Hill* link to Whistler Village. Some easy, some moderate, few difficult trails. Rides of 2-6 hours.

Valley Trail... The extensive municipal trail system which runs from Bayshores to Emerald Estates, mostly on the valley floor. Heavily used by tourists and local commuters. Easy riding.

Creekside to the Village ... Centred on rides east of Highway 99, including *Northwest Passage* and the *Mountainbike Park* (ski-lift access) on Whistler Mountain. Includes *Blueberry* trail, *Little Spearhead* and *Valley Trail*. 1-3 hours rides.

Village to Green Lake... Many short trails in this extensively-developed area near the site of Whistler Village and the base of Blackcomb, mostly in the easy to moderate grades, and never far from the Village amenities. *Cut Yer Bars* offers short harder rides off Lorimer Road. *Lost Lake* is the biggest and most popular trail network in Whistler, an excellent place for first-timers and families. This is the best place to go if you are new to the area and West Side Trails are too long or daunting. Rides of ½ hour to a half day.

West Side ... For expert riders, West Side is what "fat tire dreams are made of." These rides, generally strenuous climbs followed by steep descents, are centred on the steep hillsides above Alta Lake Road, which travels north-south along the valley, roughly parallel to Highway 99 on the west side of Alta Lake. Includes such Whistler classics as *A River Runs Through It* and *Binty's,* and the adjacent trail network of *Mel's Dilemma*. 1-2 days total riding.

Green Lake — Shadow Lake ... Characterised by several strenuous and difficult trails above Highway 99 between Alpine Meadows and the Wedgemount Parking lot, fine loop rides around Green Lake and Cougar Mountain, and the Forest Service Trail network at Shadow Lake. 1-2 days total riding.

62

Recommended Rides

Chance Creek - Function Junction

🟢 **1-1½ hours.** Chance Creek FSR at Highway 99 to Pinecrest. Return the same way or along the highway.

🟢 **1½-2 hours.** Brandywine Falls to Function Junction, either direction. Return the same way or along the highway.

Upper Cheakamus Valley

🟢 **1-1½ hours.** *Riverside Trail*, return. For a longer ride (1½-2hrs), continue up to Loggers Lake and back to Function Junction via *Lower Ridge Trail* 🟦.

🟦 **1½-2½ hours.** *Riverside Trail* to Basalt Valley Road; back to Function Junction along *Upper* and *Lower Ridge Trail*. Allow for some difficult riding on the upper trail, other wise easy to moderate trails.

🟦 ❤️ **3-4 hours.** The full tour of the Upper Cheakamus. Up *Microwave Hill*, down *Highline*. Follow Eastside Main to the *Cheakamus Lake Trail*; cross the river; back along the *Helm Creek Trail*, up Basalt Valley Road and return to Function Junction along *Ridge Trail*.

Creekside to the Village

🟢 **1-2 hours.** *Little Spearhead*.

🟦 **½-1 hour.** *Blueberry Trail*.

🟢 🟦 **2-6 hours.** *Whistler Backroads Mountainbike Park*.

🟦 **1½-2 hours.** *Northwest Passage* from Creekside, and back along the highway or the *Valley Trail*.

The Village to Green Lake

🟢 🟦 **½-4 hours.** *Lost Lake* trails.

♦ **½-1 hour.** Follow the race circuit at the base of Blackcomb.

🟦 ♦ **1-2 hours.** *Cut Yer Bars* trails.

8 Hours, 4 Litres of water, 6 powerbars later...

♦ ❤️ ❤️ ❤️ **6-12 hours.** This brilliant day out on the bike is the ultimate Whistler challenge for the fast and the honed—at least 60 kilometres, with only 3 on so on blacktop and several food stores along the way.

Start at Function Junction, head up *Millar Creek*, *Lower Sproat*, down *Beaver Pass*, *Whip Me*, *Snip Me*, up and back down *Rebob*, through *Mel's Dilemma* to Alpine Meadows. Head up *Shit Happens*, then *Section 102* and *Thrill Me, Kill Me*. Back to the Village by the *Green Lake Loop*, over *Northwest Passage* and *Microwave Hill* to Function Junction.

63

Recommended Rides

Valley Trail

🟢 If all you want to do is pedal around with the least possible difficulty, this is the place. Lots of variety. Try starting at Creekside, pedal to Green Lake, back via Lost Lake and the Village with many interesting side trips.

West Side

All West Side trails can be reached from the Village via the Valley Trail.

- 🟢 ½ hour. *Barts Dark Trail.*
- 🟦 ½-1 hour. *Whip Me, Snip Me,* to finish down the Rainbow trail.
- 🟦 1-1½ hours. *A River Runs Through It.*
- ◆ 1-1½ hours. *Ricks Roost*, from Meadow Park Sports Centre.
- ◆ ❤ 1½-3 hours. Up *Lower Sproat*, down *Beaver Pass*, up *Whip Me Snip Me*, down the Rainbow Trail to Alta Lake Road, and finish up and down *Rebob*.
- ◆ ❤ 2-3 hours. *Binty's*, and for added spice, climb up through *Mel's Dilemma*.

Green Lake to Shadow Lake

- 🟢 2-5 hours. *Soo Valley Loop*. Don't miss the Showh Lakes and Ancient Cedars side trip.
- 🟦 2-3 hours. *Green Lake Loop* from the Village. Take the Valley Trail past Lost Lake and Meadow Park to Emerald Estates, then back along the east side of Green Lake to the Village.
- ◆ 1½-2½ hours. *Thrill Me, Kill Me.*
- ◆ ❤ 3-5 hours. From the Village, ride *Shit Happens* to Emerald Estates, *Section 102*, *Thrill Me, Kill Me,* and back around Green Lake.

The Cheakamus Challenge

🟦 ❤ ❤ 5-8 hours. This famous 62 kilometre race, held in late September, runs from Cheekye north of Brackendale, to Whistler Village. Riding the entire course, or parts of it for fun is popular, offering great scenery and a day to remember if you have never ridden it before—especially the formidable amount of climbing on gravel roads. The final section from Function Junction to the Village can be avoided (no excuse necessary) to trim the effort. There is a bakery and restaurant for refuelling at Function. The winning time in 1995 was 2 hours 36 minutes. The fastest women's time is about 2 hrs 58 minutes. Needless to say, if you ride the course from Whistler to Cheekye it requires considerably less effort—you have the sun in your face and gravity in your favour.

Facilities

Coffee... Try Second Cup at the Crystal Lodge near Whistler Express Gondola; Grabba Jabba next door to Grinders in Village North, Starbucks in the Village or the Cookie Company.

Groceries... IGA Plus supermarket is the biggest in Whistler, in the Village North mall off Lorimer Road. Try also Nesters Mall on Highway 99, Food Plus at Creekside (24hr) and Alpine Meadows Market just off the highway.

Restaurants... Everything from fast food of all types and brand names, to $200 a plate. Try Auntie Ems in the Whistler Marketplace for veggie friendly fuel.

Pubs... Whistler is full of them. Try Mountain Brew House in the Village North Marketplace.

Bank Machines... About ten in all: in Alpine Meadows; Nesters Mall; Village North; Creekside; and the Village centre.

Showers... Meadow Park Sports Centre off Highway 99, just south of Alpine Meadows. The $5 drop-in fee includes skating, an exercise room, hot tub, sauna and swimming pool.

Bike Shops... There are several throughout the area, notably in Village North and the Village. Of particular interest are Grinders Bikes and Boards in the Village North, Evolution in the Village, and Whistler Backroads in the Westbrook Hotel.

Camping... Ten kilometres south of Creekside at the BC Forest Service site at Cal-Cheak. It is on the Cheakamus Challenge course and is free (for now, anyway).

Local Radio... ....Commercial radio at 107.1 FM. CBC national radio at 1260AM, and 100.1FM

Beer and Wine... Two BC government liquor stores—in the Village, and at Village North, and several private outlets.

Medical... A full facility with 24 hour on-call service at the corner of Lorimer Road and Blackcomb Way.

Mountainbike tours... A number of Whistler companies offer bike tours to suit all abilities. Call the Whistler Chamber of Commerce at 932-5528 for more information, Whistler Mountain at 932-3434 or Blackcomb at 932-3141.

Trail Ownership

The following list is intended to give an indication of the land ownership and jurisdiction of the trails in each area. The vast majority of trails in the Whistler area are on public land: crown, municipal, and provincial park. Significant areas, however are owned privately. The trails described which are privately-owned are all on undeveloped land with no nearby habitation or industrial activity, where the public has used the existing trails, in most cases, for many years. Trails believed to be on private land close to residences, industrial plants or otherwise developed commercially, have been excluded.

When out on the trails, it is no easy matter to determine jurisdiction boundaries in the absence of signage. But whether the land be privately-owned or within the public domain, the way in which the trail is used should be the same: with respect. Someone, somewhere, has responsibility to care for it and that job is made easier by minimising erosion, leaving no garbage, respecting other users and observing any posted signage.

Chance Creek to Pinecrest... Crown, BC Hydro, and some undeveloped private land.

Brandywine to Function Junction... BC Parks, crown land, municipal, BC Rail and undeveloped private.

Upper Cheakamus Valley... Municipal, crown land, and BC Parks.

Creekside to the Village... Municipal, Whistler Mountain Ski Corporation, crown land, and undeveloped private land.

The Village to Green Lake... Municipal, Blackcomb Skiing Enterprises.

West Side... Municipal, undeveloped private land and crown land.

Green Lake to Shadow Lake... Municipal, undeveloped private land, and crown land.

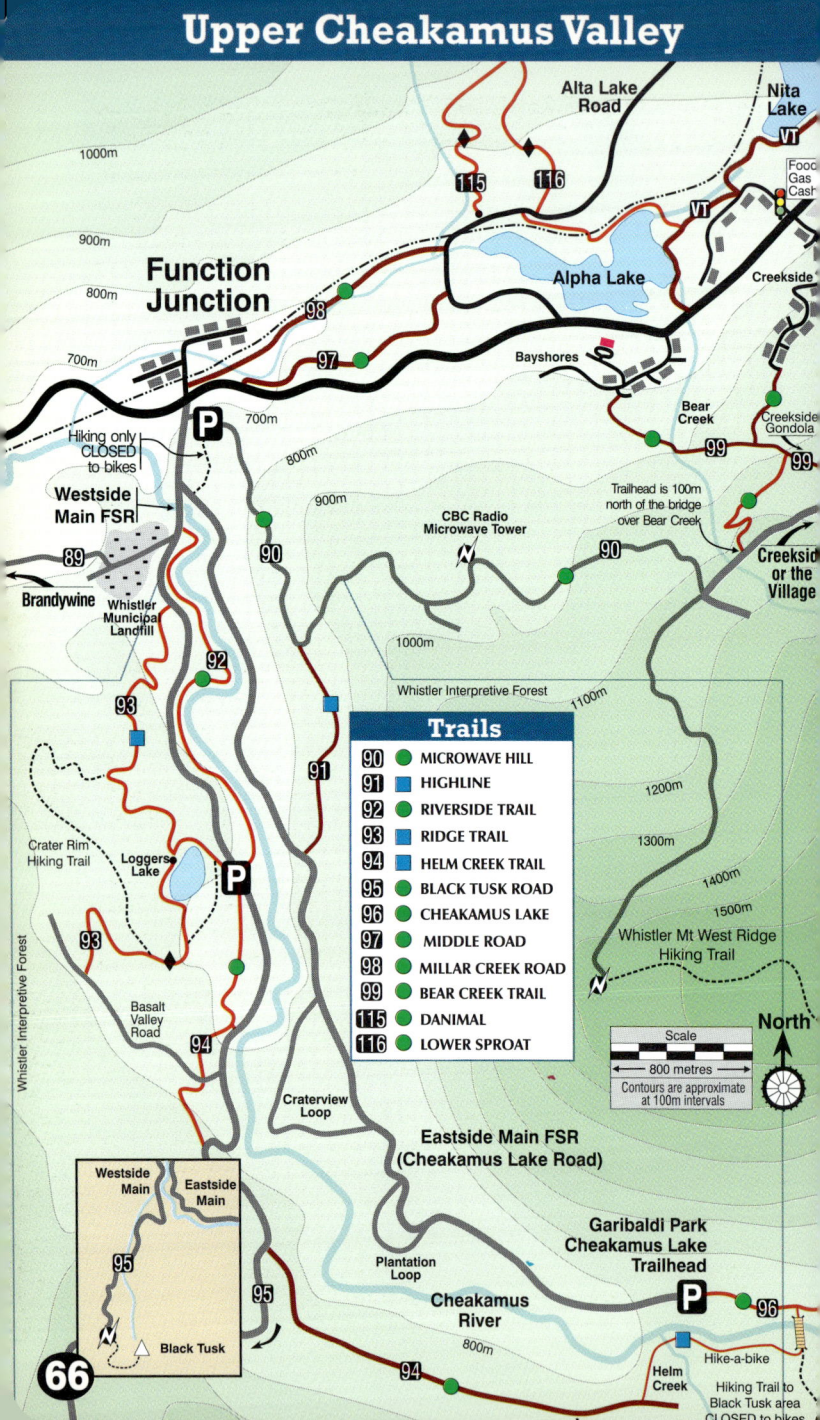

Upper Cheakamus Valley

Covering a wide area south of Creekside, and east of Highway 99 in the upper Cheakamus River valley, these trails encompass the Whistler Interpretive Forest, where the BC Forest Service has built a useful network. Expect to find hikers in the Loggers Lake area and on the very popular trail to Cheakamus Lake in Garibaldi Park, so use caution approaching blind corners and when passing.

The most convenient parking area for riding is just off the east side of Highway 99, opposite the entrance into the Function Junction industrial area. The Cheakamus Challenge race passes through this parking lot before climbing over the legendary *Microwave Hill*, *Bear Creek Trail* and *Northwest Passage* en route to the finish line in Whistler Village. And, for those who really want it, the ride up into the alpine west of the Black Tusk is one of the most strenuous listed in this guide.

90 Microwave Hill      1½-2hrs
Although this is the most feared hill on the Cheakamus Challenge racecourse, it is by no means the hardest climb in this guide. Starting from Function Junction, a good road with some brutally steep and occasionally loose sections leads over the hills to Creekside. Over the years, thousands of riders in the Challenge race have gallantly struggled up this famous hill near the end of the race, hence its well deserved reputation for bonking and suffering. After passing the infamous microwave tower, the road descends before more climbing with rewarding views of the valley leads to a major junction. Don't go right, it takes you much higher to another microwave tower far up the hill. Turn left and cross Bear Creek, then left into the trees and down a fast singletrack descent to the *Bear Creek Trail*. Descend to Creekside from here, or go right up the *Bear Creek Trail* to the Creekside Gondola and on to the Village via *Northwest Passage*. The time given is to Creekside. Allow another half hour or more to the Village.

91 Highline
Twenty to thirty minutes of pedalling up *Microwave Hill* from the parking lot at Function Junction leads to this rolling doubletrack descent to Eastside Main. Leave *Microwave Hill* at the first major bend to the left.

92 Riverside Trail
As the name implies, this trail hugs the south bank of the Cheakamus River, with fine viewpoints from which kayakers can often be seen at play. The lower half of the trail is a warm up for the short, steep climbs which follow.

Lost Lake Trails. Rider unknown.
Photo: Elizabeth Swan, Coast Mountain Photography

UPPER CHEAKAMUS VALLEY

93 Ridge Trail Upper ◆ and Lower ■ 1-1½hr
For the lower, easier section from Loggers Lake down toward Function Junction, head up the short link from the Westside Main parking area to the trailhead. Starting up Basalt Valley Road offers a longer, but technically harder ride. Fun, twisting singletrack.

94 Helm Creek Trail ● 2-2½hr
This ride links several trails, and offers a few choices for length. Best ridden clockwise. The western end is generally easy, but the eastern end demands 20 minutes of very difficult hike-a-biking between Helm Creek and the footbridge over the Cheakamus River. Follow the trail from the Westside Main parking area near Loggers Lake, cross Basalt Valley Road, and follow a grassy road which deteriorates into a rough (*really* rough) hike-a-bike track to Helm Creek. Cross the Cheakamus River on the footbridge.

95 The Black Tusk ●   5-7hr
A long, arduous, but scenic trek up Westside Main—a steep and often rough road which leads high into the alpine west of the Black Tusk, ending at a big microwave station. This is a prize worth boasting about, especially if you start at Function Junction, ride to the microwave station, hide your bike, and run up to the summit of the Black Tusk.

96 Cheakamus Lake ● 1-1½hr
Of the few multi-use trails that lead into Garibaldi Park, this is the most contentious. ***Please be careful!*** Hikers out for a relaxing stroll do not mix well with mountain-bikers-in-a-hurry. Continued conflict could result in the trail being closed to cyclists. Better to leave the bike behind and walk.

97 Middle Road   (The Expo Trail) ●
A good choice when heading from Whistler Village to Function Junction, starting off the south end of Alta Lake Road, this drier alternative to Millar Creek Road can be found just before a sharp bend to the left.

98 Millar Creek Road ●
Prone to flooding. Follow the tracks off Alta Lake Road to join with this speedy doubletrack. Easily ridden in either direction.

Be courteous to other trail users. They like to be there too, and everyone's day is more pleasant with a smile or a wave.

Creekside to the Village

This area covers trails between Creekside and the Village, and east of the Valley Trail. Bayshores, near Creekside is the southern end of the Valley Trail—a major recreational route through the entire valley which extends as far north as Emerald Estates. Park by the highway in Creekside, or in the Village area, depending on your choice of trail.

99 Bear Creek

This trail provides a link from Creekside and Bayshores to either the southern end of *Northwest Passage* or the northern section of *Microwave Hill*. Going up, follow Gondola Way Rd to its end, then a wide, steepish trail beyond. Keep left at the first fork, (going right at the second fork takes you south over *Microwave Hill* to Function Junction) up to a major gravel road (steep). Left here, then immediately right leads up to the Gondola Access Road, down under the Creekside Gondola and the start of *Northwest Passage*. See the map on page 78.

VT Valley Trail

This major recreation and commuter route provides a fine off-road link between most areas of Whistler. It is scarcely possible to ride a bike in Whistler and avoid it, so visitors are well advised to get familiar with its layout. Currently, the Valley Trail totals about 40 kilometres in all, and althought it was a visionary development when first began in the 1980s, it has since become plagued by intense crowding, especially on holiday weekends in summer. Be very careful of mad roller bladers, timetrialing roadies, innocent tourists, dogs, cats, bears, and oblivious runners with walkmans. Spare a special thought for baby strollers, as the occupants will probably be riding the trails with you in a few years.

100   Northwest Passage   1-1½hr

This popular, heavily used trail connects Creekside and the Village. South to north is usually preferred. From Creekside, climb up the Gondola Access Road or *Bear Creek Trail* to the crossing under the Creekside Gondola. Head north from here along pleasant, open singletrack, steep in places. To avoid The Wall (you'll know it when you get there) a convenient singletrack escapes down to Brio. Otherwise, bash on to join the Whistler Mountain Access Road. Please avoid going down this road, better by far to go uphill for 10 metres, then left onto singletrack, and down to the Village.

101   Blueberry Trail

A popular and heavily-used trail between Alta Vista and Tapley's Farm, and a great warm up for some of the longer rides.

Over the logs in Cut Yer Bars — riders unknown   Photo: Bonny Makarewicz

Ken Marler racing on Cactus Cut.
Photo: Rob Cocquyt.

Willie Whistler
Photo: Bonny Makarewicz

CREEKSIDE TO THE VILLAGE

102 Mountainbike Park 🟢 🟦   2-6hrs

This trail network on the northern slope of Whistler Mountain above the Village, is the only user-pay trail system in this guide, operated by Whistler Backroads Adventures in conjunction with Whistler Mountain Ski Corporation. Trails were developed specifically for mountainbikers and range from Easy to Moderate. Needless to say, most of them head downhill. If you are willing to pay to be whisked up the Whistler Express Gondola to the Olympic mid-station, it is a pretty good deal. Once there, sweatless, a number of choices lie in store.

For those new to mountain biking, try the *Crabapple Trail* (well signed) or the meadows of *Fantastic*, both of which take you down ski runs to the base. If a more technical and woodsy ride is sought, a good choice is to follow *Root Rutabaga*, or through the *Badlands* and *Blueberry Crumble*. The latter three trails collectively make up *The Golden Triangle*, generally tight, with shady paths through thickets of young alder. Expect to see many more trails developed here in the future.

Get your tickets at the Whistler Mountain ticket booths at the base of the Whistler Express lift.

103 Little Spearhead 🟢   1-2hrs

This friendly 12km loop starts at the Village from Blackcomb Way, and heads up the Singing Pass road to the hikers parking lot. Head left out of the far corner of the overflow parking lot and wind down for a kilometre or so of worry-free, non-technical fun to a log bridge over Fitzsimmons Creek, followed by an easy ride to join the the Blackcomb Mountain service road back to the Village. Watch for traffic and control your speed as this can be a very busy road.

No Pat's

No Pat's is the holy grail of mountain bike trails for the Whistler cognoscenti. Few have had the opportunity to ride it, fewer still have survived unscathed. It is a plunge into another reality—a scratch in the earth where hammerheads seek Nirvana. *No Pat's* stands alone, not something you can be led to by a guidebook. If you are worthy of this trail, you will hear it calling and find it—destiny. Some have said that successfully riding *No Pat's* is the next step of the Karma equation, others say it is impossible, perhaps the truth lies somewhere between.

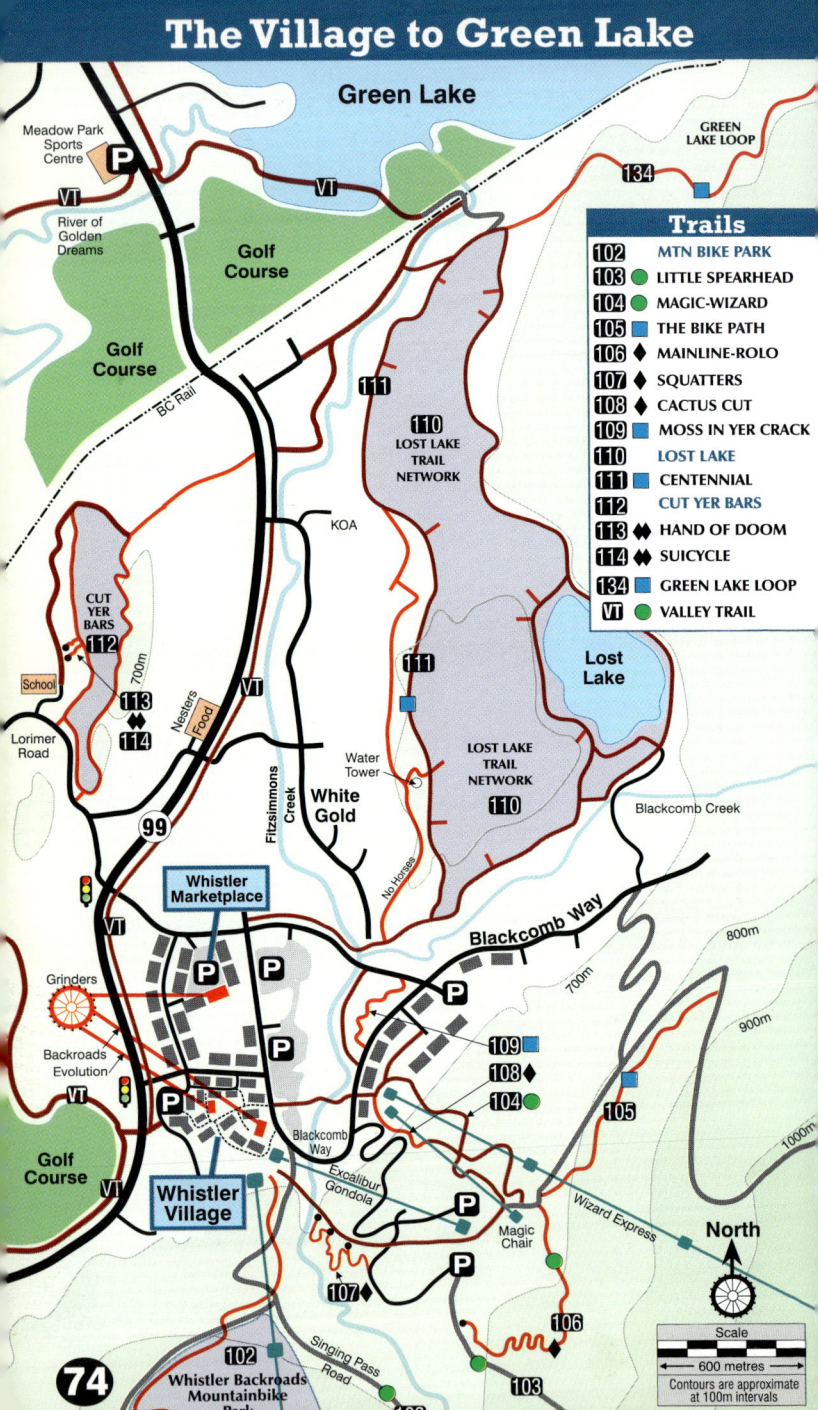

The Village to Green Lake

These trails are good choices for riders new to the area and who wish to go exploring for a while, or for those who lack the time or energy for a longer ride. While most are just as enjoyable as some of the more distant trails, the village trails are much more likely to be crowded. However, on the upside, riding around here means you are never far from a java fix, or a good Whistler brew. Lost Lake offers an extensive network of good trails close to the Village, providing hours of fun on easy and intermediate level trails—a good place for your first visit to Whistler. The trail system east of the Village, on the lower slopes of Blackcomb Mountain can make an excellent, if strenuous clockwise loop ride that packs a lot of variety—often used for mountainbike races. Start at base of the Wizard ski lift, and follow the track which climbs steeply on the left of the liftline.

104   Magic—Wizard   ●
This winding track lies to the left (north) of the Wizard Express lift and climbs up to the open area at the top of the Magic Chair.

105   The Bike Path   (Roam n' the Loam)   ■
From the open area near the top of the Magic Chair, head north along a wide road. 100m after an obvious switchback to the right, head right down tight singletrack which leads back to the start.

106   Mainline   ● —Rolo Coaster   ◆
Start near the top of the Magic Chair and climb with deceptive steepness up a wide, open swath of ski run until it drops off right into the trees and the start of *Rolo Coaster*. Tight and sustained, this rooty trail twists down with lots of fun, crossing an open area before a final descent onto a road. Go right into a huge parking lot, then left down to *Squatters*.

107   Squatters   ◆
This tight trail has three sections. Ride any or all of them. The central one is the hardest. Following on from *Rolo Coaster*, head 200 metres down the blacktop road from the parking lot, go left onto a singletrack which pops out after a few minutes at the edge of a wide, steep trail (a ski run). A left turn shortly before this point gains steeper terrain and a lower exit to the ski run. Go left again down a rocky path to Fitzsimmons Creek and up a short hike to finish back on the ski run. Head up the ski run trail back to the top of the Magic Chair and head down *Cactus Cut* to finish.

108   Cactus Cut   ◆
Head easily down from the top of the Magic Chair until the trail enters the trees. Steep, tight and rooty, it exits at the base of the Magic Chair

The start line, Cactus Cup Criterium race.   Photo: Guillaume Tessier, Coast Mountain Photography

High in the alpine on Whistler Mountain: Photo: Bonny Makarewicz

THE VILLAGE TO GREEN LAKE

109   Moss in yer Crack
This short tight singletrack runs parallel to Blackcomb Way from Lorimer Road, joining Blackcomb Way just north of the pedestrian underpass.

110   Lost Lake   2-4hrs
Lost Lake offers the biggest network of trails in the Whistler area, close to the Village with hours of fun on easy and intermediate level trails—a good place to head for on your first visit. The Valley Trail borders this area along the eastern edge, and is a useful reference point. For those who need more excitement, there are a number of short, rocky variations lurking within this playground. Go find them. Many intersections and trail junctions sport neat maps signs of the "You Are Here" variety, and trails are graded for nordic skiing, so despite the name, it is hard to get really lost. Should that happen, remember that the Valley Trail borders the network on the east, and Centennial on the west. Lost Lake Park is a great place to cool off in summer heat, or work on your tan.

Access into the area is via the Village at the south, or the Valley Trail at Green Lake in the north

111   Centennial
This north-south trail down the western edge of the Lost Lake Trails makes a stiffer, but more interesting alternative to the Valley Trail. When at the high point near a prominent water tower, a trail junction offers a better finish down to Lorimer Road via *No Horses*, or a rooty and rocky trail back northward to eventually join *Centennial* again.

112   Cut Yer Bars   1-2hrs
An extensive web of technical singletrack north of Lorimer Road, between Myrtle Phillip School and Highway 99. You can expect to find many variations. Those who seek a quick trials fix need look no further, as many of the paths are extremely technical.

The most frequently used entrance is off Lorimer Road, at the junction with Nesters Road.

113   Hand of Doom
From the rocky outcrop at the top of *Cut Yer Bars* there are two inobvious trails which drop to the school below. Looking down, this is the righthand line, a rocky, technical plunge that will challenge the most honed of riders.

114   Suicycle   ◆◆
Another relentlessly steep double diamond testpiece with intimidating log drops and rock steps. Good luck.

West Side South

Trails

99	♦	BEAR CREEK
100	■	NORTHWEST PASSAGE
115	♦	DANIMAL
116	♦	LOWER SPROAT
117	♦	BEAVER PASS
118	●	WHIP ME SNIP ME
VT		VALLEY TRAIL

North

Scale: 400 metres
Contours are approximate at 100m intervals

Rainbow Park
Satellite Dishes
Scotia Creek
Youth Hostel
Alta Lake
Fire Hydrant
Beaver Lake
Wayside Park
BC Rail
Nordic Estates
Nita Lake
Sproat Creek
BC Rail Station
Food Gas Cash
Whistler Creekside
Creekside Gondola Access R
Creekside Gondola
Alpha Lake Park
Gondola Way Road
Alpha Lake
Bayshores
78
To Northwest Passage

West Side Road

West Side trails are what fat tire dreams are made of. The vast majority of rides begin with lung searing climbs and finish with spectacular descents. As you grunt and groan in sheer agony up a merciless climb typical of the West Side, try to keep in mind the rich rewards that await you at the top.

"West Side" refers to the west side of the valley, where the trails are centred on Alta Lake Road, parallel to Highway 99 on the west side of Alta Lake. The southern end of Alta Lake Road is the first intersection off Highway 99 when coming from Function Junction, and the northern end branches off Alpine Way, north of the village. Several links with the Valley Trail make West Side accessible from Creekside and the Village.

115 Danimal ◆   1hr
This trail is divided into three distinct sections, and as a result, is rarely ridden in its entirety. The northern third is best ridden in a northerly direction from *Lower Sproat* towards *Whip Me Snip Me*. The middle section is ridable in either direction, but has numerous short hike-a-bikes. The southern section is an unforgettable descent with some unforgiving switchbacks.

116 Lower Sproat ◆   1hr
Best ridden north to south, crossing *Danimal* twice, at the boundaries of that trail's three sections. A solid 15 to 20 minute climb up a rough road leads to a small trail on the left (about 100 metres before several satellite dishes at the end of the road). The undulating singletrack which follows turns steep and fast as it heads down to Alpha Lake.

117 Beaver Pass ◆
Follow *Lower Sproat* from its north end, then 50 metres before the satellite dishes, take a doubletrack on the right. Another 5 minutes of hard climbing is followed by a fine technical descent. About two-thirds of the way down, the trail crosses *Whip me Snip Me*, but just blast straight through for an off-fall line finish.

118 Whip me Snip Me — Rainbow Trail ■
One hundred and fifty metres north of the Whistler Youth Hostel is an obvious gravel road which gives a pleasant climb for ten to fifteen minutes, offering great views of Rainbow Park and Alta Lake. Start the descent down the lower part of *Rainbow Trail* back to Alta Lake Road at a concrete building. Numerous variations allow you to choose a level of difficulty to match your mood. A more direct but less enjoyable climb to the top of *Rainbow Trail* starts through the cemetary gates on Alta Lake Road.

West Side North

Trails

- **101** 🟦 BLUEBERRY
- **112** CUT YER BARS
- **113** ♦♦ HAND OF DOOM
- **114** ♦♦ SUICYCLE
- **117** ♦ BEAVER PASS
- **118** 🟢 WHIP ME SNIP ME
- **119** 🟦 A RIVER RUNS TH. IT
- **120** 🟢 BART'S DARK TRAIL
- **121** ♦ REBOB
- **123** EMERALD FOREST
- **124** MEL'S DILEMMA
- **125** ♦♦ MANDATORY SUICIDE
- **126** ♦ BINTY'S
- **127** ♦ RICK'S ROOST
- **128** ♦ THE SCRATCH
- **VT** VALLEY TRAIL

North

Scale: 500 metres
Contours are approximate at 100m intervals

Trailheads in a wide clearing
Ricks Roost viewpoint
Alpine Way
Building
700m
800m
900m
1000m

126 4 minute climb — Turn left

125 Forest Ridge Drive

124 MEL'S DILEMMA

Meadow Park Sports Centre

River of Golden Dreams

Alta Lake Road (West Side Road)

121

21 Mile Creek

Rainbow Lake Trail

120

121

P

The Log Bridge

119

Cemetary †††

118

123 EMERALD FOREST TRAILS

112 CUT YER BARS TRAILS

♦♦ **113**
♦♦ **114**

Myrtle Phillip Elementary School

Tapleys Farm

Lorimer Road

Tapleys Farm
Crabapple

Whistler Cay

Golf Course

117

80

Alta Lake

101

99

119 A River Runs Through it ■

Although parts of of this trail were voluntarily closed by WORCA in 1996 to protect environmentally sensitive wetland, the remaining section is a deservedly popular technical testpiece for anyone who enjoys well built and challenging obstacles. Riding over the infamous log bridge spanning 21 Mile Creek, (it can be easily walked), is one of the most intimidating and potentially wettest propositions in the area. The most pleasant approach to the start of the trail is via *Bart's Dark Trail* from the north.

120 Bart's Dark Trail ●

A friendly downhill pedal (or an easy climb) parallel to Alta Lake Road, north of Twenty One Mile Creek. Start the descent 50 metres south of the *Rebob* exit. A well hidden entrance eventually opens up onto a fast old road descent.

121 Rebob Trail ◆

A stiff climb is what you pay for this popular descent. Start up a singletrack (an old road) 50 metres north of Twenty-One Mile Creek and the Rainbow Lake trailhead. *Surf's Up* heads off right just before *Rebob* bends around to the left. A little higher, where more climbing continues to the right, *Rebob* drops off to the left and heads back down to rejoin the lower section. Then, turn downhill for 25 metres to an inobvious path on the left which drops steeply downhill to a trail which parallels Alta Lake Road. Twisting and bending, the fun's never ending.

122 Surf's Up

When climbing up *Rebob*, at about 50m before a major bend to the left is the start of the now-closed *Surf's Up*. Please do not attempt this trail, as repeated skidding down the steep hillside has turned it into an ugly environmental mess which further riding will only make worse.

123 Emerald Forest ● ◆   ½-1hr

With something to offer everyone, Emerald Forest is a great place to go and get lost. Don't bother asking where you are or what you are riding, just spin those wheels. **Development in this area may be pending however, so please observe any posted signage.** The most commonly-used northern access into this area is on an obvious gravel road, a short distance south of the Valley Trail junction, and from the south, at a big gravel pit just beyond Lorimer Road.

124 Mel's Dilemma ● ◆   ½-1hr

A technically diverse maze of assorted trails, with a common start and finish between Alta Lake Road and Forest Ridge Drive, in the Alpine Meadows sub-division. Enter from the Alta Lake Road directly across from the Valley Trail link, or from the end of Forest Ridge Drive.

The legendary american Ned Overend on *Cactus Cut* in the 1996 Cactus Cup race. A former world champion, he is still one of the best riders on the planet in his early 40s.
Photo: Bonny Makarewicz

WEST SIDE 83

125 Mandatory Suicide ◆◆
Start at the top of Alpine Way in Alpine Meadows, and climb southward for about 250 metres before descending a steep, rocky, technical section. Then take the first left down an exceedingly steep 100m plunge which spits you out at Forest Ridge Drive. Serious!

126 Binty's ◆   2-3hrs
A West Side classic with great views of Whistler Mountain, Blackcomb and the peaks beyond in Garibaldi Park, *Binty's* demands a positive attitude. You have to be willing to put up with a long painful climb, a fair bit of hike-a-bike, and a shoe eating bog before you will come to realize why this trail is so popular. In short, it is an uphill grind followed by a technical downhill that never seems to end. That's what *Binty's* is all about. Start on Alpine Way and continue beyond the blacktop. The road eventually becomes a trail, and you are off on your *Binty's* adventure. Much later, halfway down the descent is a fork. Go left (uphill) for a few minutes, turn right and barrel on to finish down *Rebob* or *Surf's Up*.

127 Rick's Roost ◆
At a major clearing half way up the ascent on *Binty's*, you have the option of bailing out of the climb and taking this obvious descent on the left. Just as enjoyable as *Binty's*, but significantly shorter.

128 The Scratch ◆
In the same clearing where *Rick's Roost* is found, a small trail can be seen heading through the bushes to the right. Best described as a spicier version of *Rick's Roost,* with an impressive log and lumber bridge spanning a dry gully at the end. Steep.

Kids race action on Northlands Boulevard
Photo: Kevin McLane

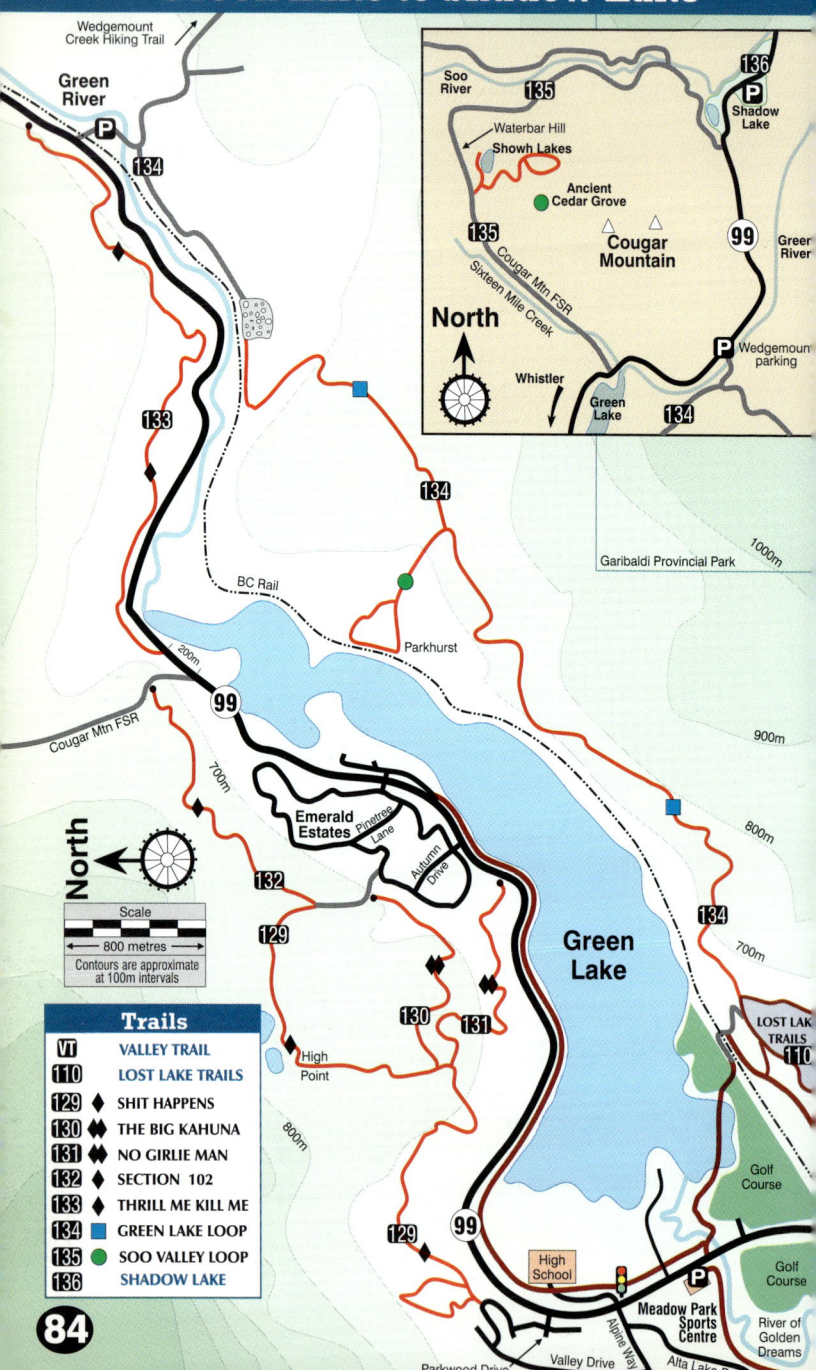

Green Lake to Shadow Lake

A number of fine loop options can be devised in this area, particularly the Cougar Mountain—Soo Valley ride, and any one of several choices, clockwise or counter-clockwise around Green Lake.

North of Green Lake is a classic Whistler trail, *Shit Happens* (noted on some maps as *It Happens*), which traverses high above Highway 99 from Alpine Meadows to Emerald Estates. Along the way, there are two very steep, burly descent variations to Emerald for the way honed. Park at the Meadow Park Sports Centre, or near Emerald Estates, depending on your choice of trail and direction. A carefully-planned combination of rides can make a great day out.

At the northern extremity of this guide, the BC Forest Service has developed a set of trails in the Shadow Lake Demonstration Forest, about halfway between Pemberton and Whistler on Highway 99.

129 Shit Happens   ◆   1½-2hr
Heed the name. This trail traverses high above Highway 99 between Emerald Estates and Alpine Meadows. From Emerald Drive at the highway, climb up Pinetree Lane, cross Emerald again and take a gravel road for about a kilometre. Keep left at a fork (Section 102 goes right), and head off south on your *Shit Happens* adventure of descents, hike-a-bikes, mud, rocks and roots, eventually reaching Parkwood Drive in Alpine Meadows. Riding south-north is also possible, but less enjoyable. Steep (*way* steep) and hard, hard, descents are possible into the Emerald Estates area down *Big Kahuna*, and *No Girlie Man*. The time is a return loop on Highway 99.

130 The Big Kahuna   ◆◆
This major, and very difficult descent links *Shit Happens* directly to Emerald Estates. When heading south from the twin lakes, look for the exit on the left, about half a kilometre after the high point.

131 No Girlie Man   ◆◆
Similar in character to *The Big Kahuna*, the trailhead is about 100m downhill from the start of that trail. Exit onto Highway 99 south of Emerald.

132 Section 102   ◆
This sinuous, rolling trail descends from above Emerald Estates to the Cougar Mountain FSR. An interesting technical approach to *Thrill Me, Kill Me*. Start up from Emerald as for *Shit Happens*, go right at the first fork.

GREEN LAKE TO SHADOW LAKE

133 Thrill Me, Kill Me   1½-2½hr

A great trail which, at present is arguably the best new ride in Whistler. Start 150m north of the Cougar Mtn FSR and traverse just above the Highway to a point 2km north of the Wedgemount Lake parking lot. Continuous climbs and descents, all ridable. The time is a return loop on Highway 99.

134 Green Lake Loop    2-4hrs

This great loop ride can be ridden in either direction, but is best clockwise. Starting from the Meadow Park Sports Centre, a number of choices are available, the easiest of which is to follow the Valley Trail to Emerald Estates, Highway 99 to the Wedgemount Parking Lot and then back south along the east side of Green Lake to Meadow Park, on a loose rocky double track with good climbs, good descents, and good views. A sandy descent halfway along the east side of the lake takes you down to Parkhust, an abandoned sawmill. Difficulty can be piled on by riding any or all of *Shit Happens*, *Section 102* and *Thrill Me, Kill Me*, to the junction with Highway 99 near Wedgemount.

135 Soo Valley Loop   3-5hrs

A fine 25 km loop which climbs up Sixteen Mile Creek on old roads over the south side of Cougar Mountain, down to the Soo River Valley and back out to Highway 99. Start up Cougar Mountain FSR, about 12 km north of Whistler on Highway 99, just beyond Emerald Estates. Steady climbing up a gravel road leads in about 5 km to a junction with the Showh Lakes—Ancient Cedars area, a well worthwhile side trip, a step back in time to what much of the corridor would have looked like before the turn of the century. The ride up involves hike-a-bikes, but the trails around the grove are really cool. Continuing on toward the Soo River Valley, beware of the huge, bike eating water bars on the long descent which follows, they have caught more than a few riders off guard, with near catastrophic results. An easy pedal down the Soo River brings you back to Highway 99.

136 Shadow Lake

About 10 kilometres north of Emerald Estates on Highway 99 is a BC Forest Service network of six trails in the area of Shadow Lake, totalling about eight kilometres. Similar in character to the Brohm Lake trail network but smaller, trail grades are generally easy to moderate. If you are passing by, or have completed the Soo Valley Loop with energy to spare, it is a neat place to spend an hour on the bike. Lots of forest interpretive signs and trail maps.

Spend a little time working on the trails to help repair the erosion you inevitably cause.

Squamish Tick List

Easy Trails

Trail		Location		Page
2	Estuary Dykes	Estuary	☐ .. ☐	27
3	Stawamus River Dyke	Smoke Bluffs	☐ .. ☐	29
4	Triple C (Crumpit Creek Cruiser)	Smoke Bluffs	☐ .. ☐	29
5	Smoke Bluff Trail	Smoke Bluffs	☐ .. ☐	29
14	The Chicanes	Smoke Bluffs	☐ .. ☐	30
15	Leisure Centre Trail	Smoke Bluffs	☐ .. ☐	30
28	The Ring Creek Rip ... 2-2½hr	Ring Creek So.	☐ .. ☐	35
30	Ring Creek Falls Trail	Ring Creek So.	☐ .. ☐	35
32	Ring Creek North FSR	Ring Creek No.	☐ .. ☐	37
38	Elfin Lakes	Ring Creek No.	☐ .. ☐	39
39	Golf Course Dyke	Garibaldi Hlds	☐ .. ☐	41
41	Mashiter Trail	Garibaldi Hlds	☐ .. ☐	41
44	Jack's Trail	Garibaldi Hlds	☐ .. ☐	41
45	The Four Lakes Trail	Alice Lake	☐ .. ☐	43
46	Dead End Connector	Alice Lake	☐ .. ☐	43
49	Rob's Corners	Alice Lake	☐ .. ☐	45
52	Cliff's Corners	Alice Lake	☐ .. ☐	45
66	Follow Your Nose	Cheekye	☐ .. ☐	47
67	Hydro Line Road	Cheekye	☐ .. ☐	47
71	Cat Lake Loop	Cat Lake	☐ .. ☐	49
77	Brohm Ridge Alpine Loop ... 4-6hr	Cheekye	☐ .. ☐	51
78	Brohm-O-Selter	Brohm Lake	☐ .. ☐	53
79	Alder Trail	Brohm Lake	☐ .. ☐	53

Someone, somewhere, has responsibility to care for the trail you are riding on, and their job is made easier if you minimise your impact on the land, and respect other users.

Squamish Tick List

Moderate Trails

Trail		Location		Page
7	Summer's Eve	Smoke Bluffs	☐ .. ☐	29
8	Endo	Smoke Bluffs	☐ .. ☐	29
16	S &M Connector	Crumpit	☐ .. ☐	31
18	Root 99	Crumpit	☐ .. ☐	31
19	Lost Loop	Crumpit	☐ .. ☐	33
20	Really Lost Loop	Crumpit	☐ .. ☐	33
26	Five Point Hill — Northside	Crumpit	☐ .. ☐	33
27	The Far Side	Crumpit	☐ .. ☐	33
35	PowerSmart 2-3hr	Ring Creek No.	☐ .. ☐	39
36	Skookum	Ring Creek No.	☐ .. ☐	36
37	Pseudotsuga (sudo-suga)	Ring Creek No.	☐ .. ☐	37
42	Roller Coaster	Garibaldi Hlds	☐ .. ☐	41
43	Lumberjack's Trail	Garibaldi Hlds	☐ .. ☐	43
47	Dead End Loop	Alice Lake	☐ .. ☐	47
50	Ed's Bypass	Alice Lake	☐ .. ☐	45
53	Don't Tell Jude	Alice Lake	☐ .. ☐	45
54	Tracks From Hell	Alice Lake	☐ .. ☐	45
55	Mike's Loop	Alice Lake	☐ .. ☐	45
56	DeBeck's Grind	Alice Lake	☐ .. ☐	45
57	Larry's Loop	Cheekye	☐ .. ☐	47
58	George's Trail	Cheekye	☐ .. ☐	47
59	Reefer Rip	Cheekye	☐ .. ☐	47
60	Two Cycle	Cheekye	☐ .. ☐	47
61	Rusty Bucket	Cheekye	☐ .. ☐	47
62	Ursus Americanus	Cheekye	☐ .. ☐	47
64	Dump Express	Cheekye	☐ .. ☐	47
65	The Buzz Cut	Cheekye	☐ .. ☐	47
70	Here Kitty Kitty	Cat Lake	☐ .. ☐	49
73	Promenade Loop	Cat Lake	☐ .. ☐	49
80	High Trail	Brohm Lake	☐ .. ☐	53
81	Cheakamus Loop	Brohm Lake	☐ .. ☐	53
82	Bridge Trail	Brohm Lake	☐ .. ☐	53
83	Evans Ridge 3-4hr	Cheakamus Cn.	☐ .. ☐	55
85	Cheakamus Canyon Trail 2-3hr	Cheakamus Cn.	☐ .. ☐	55
86	Starvation Lake Plunge	Cheakamus Cn.	☐ .. ☐	55

Squamish Tick List

Difficult Trails

Trail		Location	Page
1	Malamute Summit	Malamute	☐ .. ☐ . 27
9	Mountain of Phlegm	Smoke Bluffs	☐ .. ☐ . 30
12	Pipe Trail	Smoke Bluffs	☐ .. ☐ . 30
13	Cougar Ridge	Smoke Bluffs	☐ .. ☐ . 30
17	Lacking Head	Crumpit	☐ .. ☐ . 31
21	Meet Yer Maker	Crumpit	☐ .. ☐ . 33
23	Five Point Hill — Southside	Crumpit	☐ .. ☐ . 33
29	Powerhouse Plunge 2-3hr	Ring Creek So.	☐ .. ☐ . 35
31	Another Man's Gold	Ring Creek No.	☐ .. ☐ . 37
34	One Man's Garbage 1-1½hr	Ring Creek No.	☐ .. ☐ . 39
40	Don't Stink	Garibaldi Hlds	☐ .. ☐ . 41
48	Rock n' Roll	Alice Lake	☐ .. ☐ . 43
51	Made in the Shade	Alice Lake	☐ .. ☐ . 45
63	The Undertaker	Cheekye	☐ .. ☐ . 47
69	Barney's Bounce	Cat Lake	☐ .. ☐ . 49
72	Catwalk	Cat Lake	☐ .. ☐ . 49
74	Hare Scramble	Cat Lake	☐ .. ☐ . 51
75	I am Canadian	Cat Lake	☐ .. ☐ . 51
76	Nine Lives	Cat Lake	☐ .. ☐ . 51

Very Difficult Trails

Trail		Location	Page
6	Banzai Pipeline	Smoke Bluffs	☐ .. ☐ . 29
10	White Bronco	Smoke Bluffs	☐ .. ☐ . 30
11	Tree Hugger	Smoke Bluffs	☐ .. ☐ . 30
22	Face of Dick	Crumpit	☐ .. ☐ . 33
24	Five Point Hill — The Raa	Crumpit	☐ .. ☐ . 33
25	Five Point Hill — Numan's Arm	Crumpit	☐ .. ☐ . 33
33	The Nineteenth Hole 2-2½hr	Ring Creek No.	☐ .. ☐ . 39
68	Catnap	Cat Lake	☐ .. ☐ . 49
84	My Trail	Cheakamus Cn.	☐ .. ☐ . 55

§

Whistler Tick List

Easy Trails

Trail		Location	Page
88	Chance Creek - Pinecrest	Chance Creek	☐..☐ 57
89	Brandywine - Function Junc. 1-2hr	Brandywine	☐..☐ 57
90	Microwave Hill 1-2hr	Cheakamus	☐..☐ 67
94	Helm Creek Trail 2-2½hr	Cheakamus	☐..☐ 69
95	The Black Tusk 5-7hr	Cheakamus	☐..☐ 69
96	Cheakamus Lake	Cheakamus	☐..☐ 69
97	Middle Road	Creekisde	☐..☐ 69
98	Millar Creek Road	Creekside	☐..☐ 69
99	Bear Creek	Creekside	☐..☐ 71
103	Little Spearhead 1-2hr	Village	☐..☐ 73
104	Magic—Wizard	Village	☐..☐ 75
120	Bart's Dark Trail	West Side	☐..☐ 81
135	Soo Valley Loop 3-5hr	Green Lake	☐..☐ 86

Moderate Trails

Trail		Location	Page
91	Highline	Cheakamus	☐..☐ 67
92	Riverside Trail	Cheakamus	☐..☐ 67
93	Ridge Trail West 1-1½hr	Cheakamus	☐..☐ 69
100	Northwest Passage 1-1½hr	Creekside	☐..☐ 71
101	Blueberry Trail	Village	☐..☐ 71
105	The Bike Path	Village	☐..☐ 75
109	Moss in yer Crack	Village	☐..☐ 77
111	Centennial	Village	☐..☐ 77
118	Whip me Snip Me — Rainbow Trail	West Side	☐..☐ 79
119	A River Runs Through it	West Side	☐..☐ 79
134	Green Lake Loop 2-4hr	Green Lake	☐..☐ 86

Trail Networks

Trail			Page
VT	Valley Trail	🟢	☐..☐ 71
102	Mountainbike Park	🟢 🟦	☐..☐ 73
110	Lost Lake	🟢 ♦	☐..☐ 77
112	Cut Yer Bars	🟦 ♦	☐..☐ 77
124	Mel's Dilemma	🟢 ♦	☐..☐ 81
136	Shadow Lake	🟢 🟦	☐..☐ 86

Whistler Tick List

Difficult Trails

Trail		Location	Page
87	The Doris Burma Memorial Trail	Chance Creek	☐ .. ☐ . 57
93	Ridge Trail East ... 1-1½hr	Cheakamus	☐ .. ☐ . 69
106	Mainline—Rolo Coaster	Village	☐ .. ☐ . 75
107	Squatters	Village	☐ .. ☐ . 75
108	Cactus Cut	Village	☐ .. ☐ . 75
115	Danimal ... 1hr	West Side	☐ .. ☐ . 79
116	Lower Sproat ... 1hr	West Side	☐ .. ☐ . 79
117	Beaver Pass ... 1hr	West Side	☐ .. ☐ . 79
121	Rebob Trail	West Side	☐ .. ☐ . 81
126	Binty's ... 2-3hr	West Side	☐ .. ☐ . 83
127	Rick's Roost	West Side	☐ .. ☐ . 83
128	The Scratch	West Side	☐ .. ☐ . 83
129	Shit Happens ... 1½-2hr	Green Lake	☐ .. ☐ . 85
132	Section 102	Green Lake	☐ .. ☐ . 85
133	Thrill Me, Kill Me ... 1½-2½	Green Lake	☐ .. ☐ . 85

Very Difficult Trails

113	Hand of Doom	Village	☐ .. ☐ . 77
114	Suicycle	Village	☐ .. ☐ . 77
125	Mandatory Suicide	West Side	☐ .. ☐ . 81
130	The Big Kahuna	Green Lake	☐ .. ☐ . 85
131	No Girlie Man	Green Lake	☐ .. ☐ . 85

§

Hand of Doom at Cut Yer Bars — Darcy Burke.
Photo: Jamie Grant

Night

Riding in the dark can be an exhilarating experience. Even the most straightforward trails take on an air of mystery and leave the rider with new levels of a funky kind of apprehension.

Night riding requires that you take precautions. Always ride with someone else. Take a back-up lighting system no matter how modest. Mini Mag-Lites will do in a pinch. Tools are just as important on a night ride as they are in daytime. Warm clothing is essential. Perhaps most important of all is a good knowledge of the area where you will be riding. A 100 watt light system with a three hour burn time won't do you much good if you end up doing circles for four hours. Pay attention to the landmarks at trail junctions. Let someone you can trust know exactly where you plan to ride and how long you plan to be. Stick to that plan. Begin with the easiest trails and as your night knowledge grows so will your options.

The following are a few suggested trails which are popular and well suited to night riding.

The Four Lakes Trail
Very enjoyable with few surprises and escape options if needed.

Brohm Lake
Well signed and graded, with options for those wishing to add spice to their ride. Be especially careful of the stairs on the High Trail!!

The Ring Creek Rip
If the moon is bright you shouldn't even need your light for the hour long climb to the top of the lava flow and the start of the trail.

Upper Cheakamus Valley
Riverside Trail and *Lower Ridge Trail*. Well signed, well graded. Bears, and probably lots of them, will keep your heart racing even on the flats.

Whip Me Snip Me - Rainbow
Easy to find and follow. Enjoy it on a moonlit night!

A River Runs Through It
A relatively harmless maze. No hurry. Flat. Have fun.

Lost Lake
A huge network of trails for all abilities. Wide pavement-like doubletrack and skinny earthen singletrack all less than five minutes from the Village.

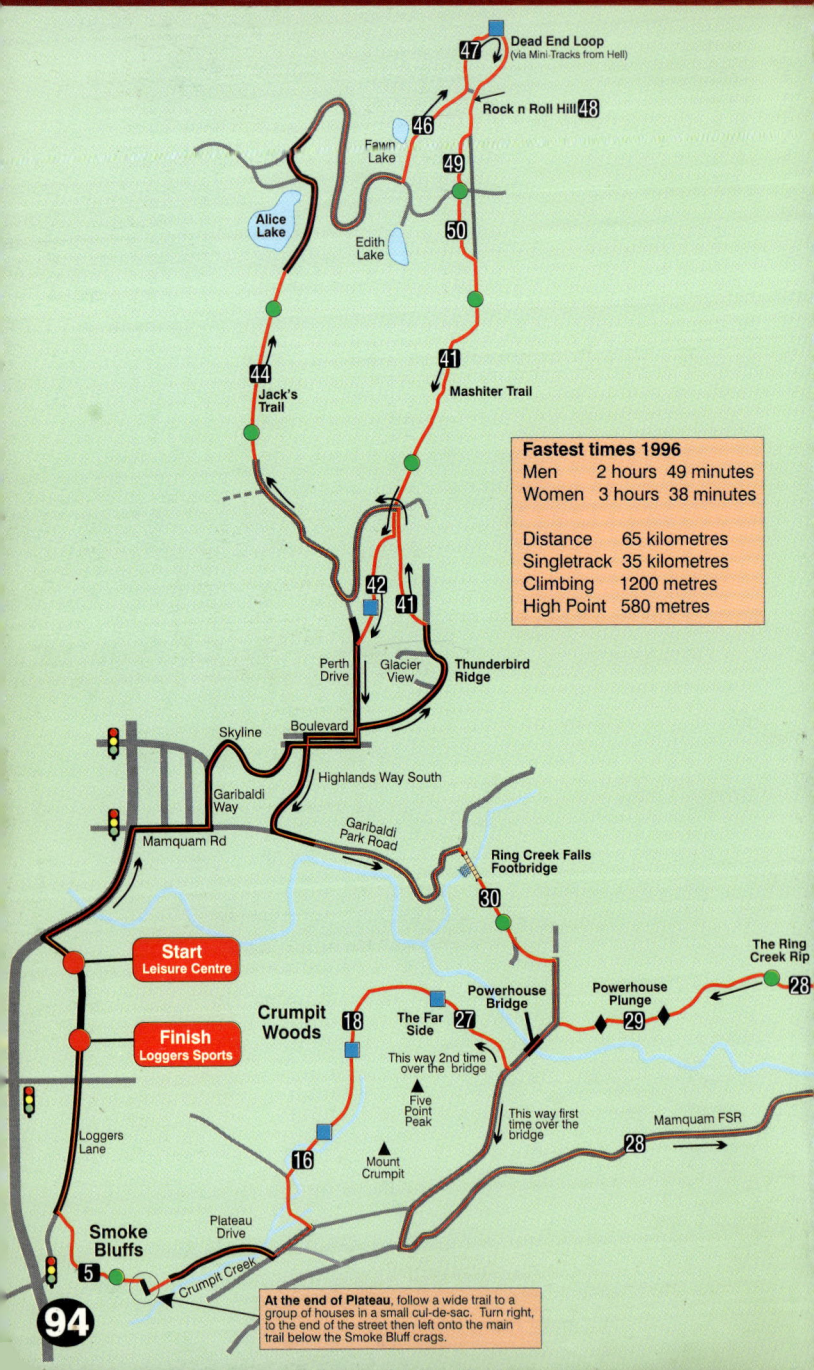